SABRINA CARPENTER

SABRINA CARPENTER

A VIBRANT JOURNEY THROUGH THE CAREER AND INFLUENCE OF A POP PRINCESS

Selena Fragassi

EPIC INK

Contents

A Short n' Sweet Introduction — 7

Part 1: Eyes Wide Open — 19

Part 2: Evolution — 53

Part 3: Prfct'ing Her Live Act — 91

Part 4: The Sabrina Show — 127

Part 5: A Busy Woman — 167

A Poetic Conclusion — 187
Discography — 194
Filmography — 196
Awards and Nominations — 198
Sources — 200
Photo Credits — 204
Acknowledgments — 206
About the Author — 207

PREVIOUS
Sabrina attends the MusiCares Person of the Year ceremony honoring Jon Bon Jovi in California, February 2, 2024.

Sabrina walking the red carpet stairs at the Met Gala in New York City, May 2, 2022.

A Short n' Sweet Introduction

In 2024, you could run, you could hide, but you could not escape the "attack of the five-foot woman." Not that anyone wanted to—she's no villain, she's Sabrina Carpenter, the alluring and hilarious pint-sized pop star who basically devoured pop culture over the course of the year, and left us all begging for a *taste* of more in any kind of sequel.

With a dizzying amount of magazine covers and centerfolds, including a spot in the *Time* 100 issue and gracing the pages of fashion and music bibles like *W* and *Rolling Stone*, plus some *SNL* spoofs and spotlights, a punchline in the opening monologue of the 2024 Emmys, a pair of viral music videos, and that MTV VMAs make out sesh with an alien, Sabrina was *everywhere*. If she wasn't on everyone's TikToks and timelines, then she was probably on her way to almost every town across America with her headline-making Short n' Sweet Tour, performing all of the hit-making songs that made her a household name over the year.

> "She's Sabrina Carpenter, the alluring and hilarious pint-sized pop star who basically devoured pop culture over the course of the year."

Sabrina performs onstage during the 67th Annual Grammy Awards in California, February 2, 2025.

By the end of 2024, Sabrina's jacked-up song "Espresso" nearly nabbed Spotify's most-streamed song award (before it was kicked off by Billie Eilish's "Birds of a Feather" in a last-minute update). The song's popularity even led to a Dunkin' collab with the chain's special menu item, Sabrina's Brown Sugar Shakin' Espresso. "I never knew that people had such a caffeine addiction . . . I underestimated how much of a problem it is in our world," she chided during her *Tiny Desk* concert.

Written with go-to collaborators Amy Allen and Steph Jones, "Espresso" nearly didn't become the platinum single it was destined to be. "I was completely alone in wanting to release 'Espresso.' Not so much from my immediate team. But when it came to 'the powers above,' there was a lot of questioning behind whether it made sense," she told *Variety*. "But they trusted me in the end, and I was happy that I believed in myself at that moment."

The idea for the track percolated in Sabrina's head while in France, months before she would appear sipping on a double shot in a series of promos for the summer 2024 Paris Olympics. A moment of inspiration came when she had a break from opening Taylor Swift's Eras Tour and had some time off to vacation in Europe, where she was drawn into the city's café culture. "I was in a ghost town that had one little creperie down the road. I had my shot of espresso . . . and before I knew it the song was written," Sabrina told *W* Magazine. "It's like fate. You have to be at the right place at the right time."

"I was in a ghost town that had one little creperie down the road. I had my shot of espresso... and before I knew it the song was written."

That would become a strong theme as 2024 played out for the pop princess. As Sabrina's sixth album was released on August 23, it was a *Short n' Sweet* ride to the top of the charts in the ensuing months. (Even if it was a long time coming for the self-described "overnight success ten years in the making.") Sabrina has been putting in sweat equity since her first EP launched in 2014 and has triumphantly overcome her share of love scandals that could have stained the reputation of any other pop star.

Yet, with some well-placed spotlights on the festival circuit, The Eras Tour, and a great promo machine behind her, Sabrina's latest love opus became the second longest-running No. 1 debut on the *Billboard* 200 chart for the year, just behind Taylor's *The Tortured Poets Department*. The twelve tracks on *Short n' Sweet* also netted three Top 10 hits, with "Please Please Please," "Taste," and "Espresso" peaking at respective Nos. 1, 2, and 3 spots on the *Billboard* Hot 100 chart. This also marked the first No. 1 hit for Sabrina in her decade-long music career.

FOLLOWING
Sabrina at the Metropolitan Museum of Art Costume Institute Benefit Gala in New York, May 4, 2024.

"I'd be lying if I said I hadn't dreamt about this day my whole life, so I am filled with gratitude."

A few short months after its release, the album picked up at critical speed on many "best of the year" lists too. *Rolling Stone* placed *Short n' Sweet* at No. 4 on its "Best Albums of the Year" roundup, calling it Sabrina's "full-on coronation album, flaunting her knack for turning romantic roadkill into flippantly brilliant pop." *Billboard* put the album in the No. 3 spot, claiming Sabrina "truly arrived with this album, delivering twelve songs that could each stand alone on pop radio while somehow never treading the same ground." *Consequence* added "Espresso" to its list of the "200 Best Songs" of 2024, at No. 8, calling it "the frothy, utterly addictive bop that morphed into a cultural habit we couldn't kick if we wanted to."

Billboard even named Sabrina the No. 2 Greatest Pop Star of 2024, just behind Kendrick Lamar. To support the honor they stated that, "after years of hard work, a string of smash hits and a no-misses album, [which] propelled Carpenter to superstardom in 2024, [it] cement[ed] her status as America's newest sweetheart." But perhaps *Salon* said it best, noting that Sabrina "emerged from the Disney Channel's ashes as a fiery, [hot] pop diva." Like the godmothers of hot pop before her—Madonna, Britney, and Christina—Sabrina's *Short n' Sweet* showed a brilliant knack for flaunting just enough innuendo to tantalize the masses, and did so unabashedly and without shame.

Another fulcrum point came when Sabrina was nominated for an impressive six grammys in November 2024, including Album of the Year and Best Pop Vocal Album for *Short n' Sweet*, Record of the Year and Best Solo Pop Performance for "Espresso," Song of the Year for "Please Please Please," and Best New Artist. "I don't know how that's possible. I'm the best *old* artist. [Shoot], I've been here," Sabrina joked regarding

---

Sabrina attends Rihanna's Savage X Fenty Show Vol. 3 in Los Angeles, California, September 24, 2021.

her "new artist" nod. (Her first single, "Can't Blame a Girl for Trying," was released way back in 2014.) Though, in another sweet moment, Sabrina posted a video of her and her touring crew wearing pj's and wrapped in fuzzy pink blankets on their bus celebrating the nominations as they were announced in real time. "I'd be lying if I said I hadn't dreamt about this day my whole life, so I am filled with gratitude," she captioned the Instagram video.

When the 67th Annual Grammy Ceremony was telecast in February 2025, Sabrina took home the honors for Best Pop Solo Performance and Best Pop Vocal Album, just moments after offering a jazzy mash-up performance of "Espresso" and "Please Please Please." In the front row, some famous supporters, including Taylor Swift, Jack Antonoff, Margaret Qualley, Billie Eilish, and Finneas, gave her a standing ovation.

Sabrina was but one in a league of women who were handsomely nominated and victorious in the '24 Grammy cycle. "Is this the Grammys' year of the woman? You'd have to say yes," said *Variety* in an editorial, noting that the buzz around female artists has been growing in recent years with an incredibly strong crop of talent that has kept up the momentum. "Was 2024 the Biggest Year Ever for Female Pop Stars?" *US Weekly* pondered, noting that it wasn't so long ago that #GrammysSoMale was a big topic of conversation in 2018 when only one female artist (Lorde) was in serious contention for the top honor of Album of the Year.

Sabrina has been caught up in a flurry of feminine energy in the music industry—in fact, when she hailed the hormone-heavy *Short n' Sweet*, an "ovulation album" on Instagram, many fans suggested it was the perfect way to wrap up a "hot girl summer." The star has not only benefitted from

> "Pop music is messier—for the better—because of Chappell Roan, Charli XCX, and Sabrina Carpenter."
> —CNN

the takeover but also helped push it forward. In an article from CNN, the outlet posited, "Pop music is messier—for the better—because of Chappell Roan, Charli XCX, and Sabrina Carpenter," citing the artists' winning penchant for realism and self-reflection. "What people really craved this year, the TikTok generation, was to see more mess and chaos in people's lives. We wanted pop stars that we were able to see the flaws within and the charisma coming out," music curator Sam Murphy shared in the story.

Sabrina, for one, has been as real as they come. Yes, she sings about common themes of love and heartbreak and wears lingerie and garters on stage, but she's also self-deprecating and the first to laugh at her own jokes. She curses like a sailor and thrives on innuendo. Coupled with her confessional lyrics and social media approachability, she's been able to crush the facade of a pop star and buff off the polish, leaving behind a raw canvas to build from—one that's become painted in a color wheel of contradictions. She's flirty but fierce, poetic yet punchy, feminine and also masculine, and short with a giant personality.

Sabrina has kept everyone guessing with her glow-up (or should we say blowup) since the days of Disney and her companion Hollywood Records albums. At only five feet (1.5 m) tall, there's much to this pint-sized pop star, and we've only scratched the surface.

FOLLOWING
Sabrina performs at Coachella Valley Music and Arts Festival, Weekend 2, Day 1 in Indio, California, April 19, 2024.

PART 1

EYES WIDE OPEN

Sabrina Annlynn Carpenter was born to be a tortoise. It's a bit ironic considering that, when she came into the world on May 11, 1999, it was actually the year of the hare in the Chinese zodiac. But what would start to manifest, specifically after she started writing music at the young age of nine, was a slow and steady pace that would eventually pay off many years—and many albums—later.

"Something that my mom always said to me as a little girl that really annoyed me was that I am the tortoise . . . that [messed me up] because, you know, throughout my life, [I was] being told, 'Sabrina, you're the tortoise, just chill . . . just slow down, it's going to be okay,'" Sabrina shared in her acceptance speech for *Variety*'s Hitmakers Rising Artist Award in 2023. "In moments of frustration and confusion, it can feel like a letdown, but it turns out it's actually a very good thing. And I've really loved getting to know the mindset of a slow rise," she added. "Knowing that I have a lot to look forward to and no matter how much I experience and how much I have under my belt, I'll always have something to learn. That's kind of where I'm at right now, I'm just learning. And I'm very grateful."

> "Knowing that I have a lot to look forward to and no matter how much I experience and how much I have under my belt, I'll always have something to learn. That's kind of where I'm at right now, I'm just learning. And I'm very grateful."

PREVIOUS
Sabrina attends the pre-Grammy Gala at The Beverly Hilton in California, February 4, 2023.

Sabrina's mom, Elizabeth, was not only right, but she was also one of many in a supportive family that cheered on the young Carpenter along the long and winding journey. In fact, one of the first "performances" Sabrina can remember–besides frequently singing "God Bless America" in her kitchen–was at the ripe age of eight when she belted out her favorite Christina Aguilera and Mariah Carey hits at a family reunion karaoke session in her native Pennsylvania. "Everyone just had way too much alcohol, so they were so fascinated by this little eight-year-old singing karaoke," she told Stars In Cars interviewer JJ Ryan in 2018. "That was so encouraging for me to be around adults that really believed in me ... They were very kind and supportive." In a chat with *CBS News Sunday Morning* in 2024, Sabrina added, "They never told me to stop singing and I think that psychologically really helped me."

Incredibly, no one else in the Carpenter family shares Sabrina's unique gift, and that has led her to often wonder where her talent originated from. For a while, Sabrina lied and told people she was a descendant of the famous '70s-era sibling duo the Carpenters as a way to make it make sense. "I always wanted to tell people that we were related because I had no other answer for where I got my voice from, or started singing from, so I would always say, you know, the Carpenters," she jokingly recalled to *Teen Vogue*. In case you're wondering, she's not related to horror scion John Carpenter either.

It did help that her parents already had their own modest experience in the world of entertainment and understood their daughter's drive to stardom. "My whole family, it was very much around performing," she told Stars In Cars. "We grew up really loving music and loving the arts." Sabrina has previously talked about how her dad, David, was in a garage rock band and would perform covers of the Canadian prog rockers Rush.

"My whole family, it was very much around performing. We grew up really loving music and loving the arts."

Her mom, Elizabeth, a chiropractor by trade, was also a trained dancer who had tried singing for a while. In fact, Sabrina's first vocal coach was handed down from Elizabeth.

"She would teach me about stage presence and teach me the classics like Etta James and Judy Garland and Patsy Cline," Sabrina shared in the Stars In Cars interview about her coach, who was in her eighties when they started working together. It's a key relationship that influenced Sabrina's fascination with everything retro and vintage, which is now a huge part of her style book. Her parents also played a significant part; she told iHeartRadio, "They educated me on the classics and that goes for music and movies and television." Then again, as Sabrina has described herself on "Eyes Wide Open," she's always been an "old soul," and there's a part of her personality that makes you think she could've totally been contemporaries with Marilyn Monroe or Greta Garbo in another timeline. Or, as *Pitchfork* has astutely said, Sabrina is just a "Gen-Z Betty Boop."

As she was soaking up music as a kid, Sabrina also started learning to play instruments, including piano, guitar, bass, ukulele, "and drums when I'm feeling rhythmic," she told *WIRED*, which gave her a greater appreciation for the inner workings of music and arrangements. By ten years of age, she was writing her first lyrics. "I would write stuff in my notebook, but it's nothing that I'd ever want anybody in the world to hear," she jokingly told *Scholastic*'s blog, *Ink Splot*. By thirteen, ideas came that she would finally take more seriously.

When she was just two years old, Sabrina started following in her mom's footsteps with dancing. "My mom put me and all my sisters in dance lessons, which was so fun," she told *WIRED*, adding it was a near-religious practice until she was about fifteen. Dancing became a part of her daily routines again during the making of the 2020 Netflix movie, *Work It*. "I was sore," she joked. Yet, picking up choreography for the second time has made her quite flexible—do you remember the splits she did at the LA stop of the Short n' Sweet Tour that broke the internet? You can thank all those dance practices for that. "I can do the splits . . . and a one-handed cartwheel," she joked in the *WIRED* chat.

There are other talents, too. One that you might've noticed if you kept watching to the end of her 2024 episode of *Hot Ones*. To distract herself from the heat of the chicken wings, Sabrina grabbed some paper and colored pencils and drew quick caricatures of herself and host Sean Evans breathing fire. "Hang it in the Louvre," Sean playfully declared. It may not have been Monet-level, but the artwork had Sabrina's stamp all over it. "I do love to draw in my free time, my grandma was an artist," she told *WIRED*. "Drawing is one of my favorite therapeutic, calming activities."

All in the Family

Sabrina grew up around a ton of feminine energy, not only with her highly influential mom and grandmother but also with her three elder sisters. "That's why I am the [jerk]," she joked with Apple Music's Zane Lowe when discussing her birth order personality. Before she came into the Carpenter clan, Sabrina was preceded by Cayla (her half-sister), then Shannon and Sarah, all of whom are incredibly talented and work in entertainment-adjacent fields, which has naturally led to family collaborations.

The eldest, Cayla, is a hairstylist and makeup artist who has often toured with Sabrina as part of her glam squad. Shannon kept up with dancing and is a sought-after choreographer (Sabrina name-drops her in the song "Skinny Dipping"). And Sarah could easily be her body double, but instead, she works as a multitalented backup singer and "pocket harmonizer" (notably on the albums *Eyes Wide Open* and *EVOLution* and at Sabrina's early tours). Sarah is also a designer (credited as the creative director for the Short n' Sweet Tour) and photographer. She's the auteur behind the popular Instagram account @dontshakethepolaroid, in which Sabrina is often her muse. The younger sibling has called Sarah

Sarah and Sabrina Carpenter pose for a picture during "FOX & Friends" All-American Concert Series in New York City, June 27, 2014.

"an iconic photographer," adding, "We love taking photos together, it's our favorite thing in the world." Sometimes, those snaps have been used for magazine features, namely for a 2020 story on Sabrina in *Teen Vogue*.

Growing up in Quakertown, Pennsylvania (before she moved to LA in 2012), Sabrina was homeschooled, a switch that came about, one, because she needed the space to be an artist: "I was already this businesswoman that was like, 'Well, I'm gonna need the time to dedicate to my career'—at ten," she told *Variety*. And two, because of the backlash Sabrina experienced from her peers in elementary school. "Ironically, I was bullied for singing," Sabrina revealed in an *Interview* magazine chat with Maya Hawke in early 2024. "I did well in school . . . but I started homeschooling really young." There was just one thing she felt she truly missed out on by not attending a traditional school like most kids her age. "I just really wanted a locker. I had this weird obsession with wanting a locker, and I never had one," she said in a 2018 interview. But being homeschooled did give her one excellent talent. On the *Zach Sang Show*, she said, "I was great at making PowerPoints."

In a 2016 interview with Radio Disney, a video crew followed Sabrina back home to Pennsylvania, capturing the then-established actress and singer retracing her first steps. "My hometown is quiet, it's very small, but when I was younger I didn't see it as that small. I thought this place was huge. I thought it went on forever," she shared, adding, "I had dreams that I wanted to reach the world universally. I thought that if I could do it starting in this town that I could do it anywhere."

As cameras followed Sabrina upstairs to her old bedroom, it was a snapshot of her early girlie years. The room was outfitted with leopard-print wallpaper, coordinating pink animal-print curtains,

> *"I had dreams that I wanted to reach the world universally. I thought that if I could do it starting in this town that I could do it anywhere."*

and zebra-striped bedding. In the footage, she picks up an old rag doll in the corner, which she had named Maggie, strums on a pink acoustic guitar, and lies on her bed while flipping through the pages of a journal filled with her primitive lyrics. "I think most of the time if I was songwriting, it was either in my bedroom or back in my backyard. And I'm still sort of the same way . . . I like to be outside because I find more inspiration outdoors," she shared.

The family house was located in the middle of the woods, which provided a natural sense of exploration and wonder. Not to mention, an extended audience of pets. "We were a cat family and they were all strays," Sabrina shared with *WIRED*, detailing the pack as Woody, Bo, Ginger, and Mocha. In an adorable home video that has since gone viral, a very young Sabrina hangs with one of the felines and shows off that intrinsic wit that would soon become her calling card. "Okay, I got this, I got this real good. I went to animal communications school, trust me, we're, like, tight," the preteen Sabrina said to the camera before turning to her pet and meowing and hissing in its face. "You see that intimidation in his eyes?! I'm deep, I'm so deep," she responded in the next frame. The original post of the home video was perfectly captioned, "I love how it's not even forced like Sabrina been strange since she gained consciousness."

Today, Sabrina has kept those animal instincts, now a mom to her beloved dog (and Instagram star) Goodwin, who was a gift for her thirteenth birthday and likely took his name after she had a short stint on the sitcom *The Goodwin Games*. She also has two British Shorthair cats, Benny and Bjorn, named in homage to members of the Swedish music group ABBA. Most of the time, the pets stay with Sabrina's mom but come to "visit" when she has time off in her busy schedule. "I'm like the cool aunt," she told Apple Music.

The Sound of Music

In addition to studies—and pets—the Carpenter house was also its own kind of charm school, filled with plenty of extracurriculars, including music. As Sabrina told Stephen Colbert in 2024 on his late-night talk show, a pivotal moment came when she heard The Beatles at a very young age, which inspired her own journey to becoming a music artist. The Fab Four remains one of her favorite groups, with the Brits' *The White Album* and their film *Across the Universe* admittedly her desert island picks. "When I was very very young, my dad played me 'Rocky Raccoon' for the first time and I was so mesmerized by that song and the songwriting of it, that I fell in love with Paul McCartney. I was convinced that [he] was my future husband," she recalled. As with many other serendipitous moments in Sabrina's life, she had the chance to meet the Beatle that got away at the 2024 MusiCares Person of the Year ceremony. It's a moment she described to Colbert as experiencing *Stranger Things*'s The Upside Down, adding that she's still "obsessed with him."

As fate would have it, when three of Sabrina's *Short n' Sweet* singles—"Taste," "Please Please Please," and "Espresso"—all placed in the Top 5 of the *Billboard* Hot 100 in the same week (September 7, 2024), she tied a record with The Beatles exactly sixty years after they accomplished the same feat in 1964.

"When I was very very young, my dad played me 'Rocky Raccoon' for the first time and I was so mesmerized by that song and the songwriting of it, that I fell in love with Paul McCartney. I was convinced that [he] was my future husband."

Sabrina added "Rocky Raccoon" to her "Playlist of My Life" curated for *Teen Vogue* in 2018, adding more detail about the first time she heard the song. "This is music?" she wondered. "To a lot of people they were probably just thinking, 'Oh The Beatles were high when they wrote this.' I mean they were high, but also there's such a story behind it and they kind of did that with all their songs, and it made me really want to be a songwriter."

Elsewhere on the playlist was Christina Aguilera's "Beautiful" ("It was one of the songs that was the most influential in my life; I've carried the message with me," Sabrina said). Etta James's "At Last" also made the cut; it was one of the first songs Sabrina ever learned to sing and play via her previously mentioned octogenarian vocal coach. Sabrina said the powerful jazzy standard taught her to "really appreciate soul and the power of a voice" and it also "led me down a path to being open to all kinds of music later in my life because I wasn't forced to like one thing."

To her point, Sabrina's at-home music education had diverse artists on repeat, such as Stevie Nicks, Dolly Parton, Carole King, and Patsy Cline, all iconic singers who admittedly reshaped her idea of a pop star. "That music didn't necessarily feel like pop to me," she told *Interview* magazine, adding, "I don't love the idea that a pop star is someone who makes catchy songs with easy-to-grasp concepts." Sabrina kept that memo close to heart as she started writing her own music, with those early inspirations and influences as wide-ranging as her now multioctave range.

By the time she was nine, just a year after cutting her chops at family karaoke, Sabrina started posting covers on YouTube of her favorite songbirds, like Adele, Taylor Swift, and Christina Aguilera, many of which gained traction as her dynamic voice started to emerge. They're still relics she can proudly stand behind, which she often does.

In fact, as views of those early YouTube videos picked up, they spread all the way to China. In particular, a cover of Josh Groban's "You Raise Me Up" was all the rage in Asia and led to Sabrina's very first TV appearance, performing on Hunan Live TV. *The Morning Call* reported that the performance was seen by approximately eleven million people. "China went crazy [for the Josh Groban cover] and invited me to perform," Sabrina recalled to *Teen Vogue*. For her debut moment, she chose Christina Aguilera's "Something's Got a Hold on Me." There was always something about Christina that made Sabrina feel safe as a budding artist. She told *Teen Vogue*, "Ever since I was little, I kind of had a very deep tone to my voice so I always thought I sounded like a man and then I'd listen to songs by Christina and I'd be like, okay I feel better."

FOLLOWING
Sabrina signs a wall at a Teen Choice Awards after-party in Universal City, California, August 11, 2013.

"Ever since I was little, I kind of had a very deep tone to my voice so I always thought I sounded like a man and then I'd listen to songs by Christina and I'd be like, okay I feel better."

Miley Becomes a Muse

With her confidence building after the Hunan Live TV performance, it was just a year later that ten-year-old Sabrina entered into a nationwide contest in 2009 hosted by none other than Miley Cyrus. The MileyWorld Superstar competition aimed to find the next big tween talent. Like many other millennials, Sabrina was an uber-fan of Miley when she was a kid–watching Miley's career gave her starry eyes for everything Disney, too.

As *Rolling Stone* reported, when Sabrina was just six years old and saw *Hannah Montana* for the first time, a light bulb went off. "I remember ... watching the pilot and being like 'I want to do that. I want to sing, and I want to act, and I want to dance. I want to do all those things," she said. In fact, seeing *Hannah Montana* showed young Sabrina that her love of singing could be something she could do when she grew up. "I was already thinking about my career at six," she joked with AOL.com in 2017. "The next four years it was basically annoying my mom and dad to take me to California."

"I want to sing, and I want to act, and I want to dance. I want to do all those things."

Sabrina was one of seven thousand entrants in the MileyWorld Superstar contest and also the youngest one to make it to the Top 4 after submitting covers of some of her favorites like The Beatles's "Come Together." As part of the final round, she and the other hopefuls were tasked with making a video of the Miley/Hannah Montana song, "Hoedown Throwdown," with fans voting for their favorites on Miley's website.

In her submission, Sabrina, looking like a total angel in long pigtails and a pink vest, begins by introducing herself with a slight lisp: "Hi, my name is Sabrina, I'm ten years old . . . I just want to thank everyone for getting me into the Top 10, and we had a lot of fun with this video, so I hope you enjoy." The shaky camcorder piece starts with the young Carpenter opening the door to her family's stone house as one of the stray cats runs out. Sabrina and her two sisters huddle on the family's front walkway before the youngest sister starts teaching them the choreography for the dance. A few frames later, the video pans inside a club where little Sabrina is leading a line of cowboy-hat-donning dancers. Even at a young age, Sabrina's pitch was pristine, and her choreography a sure shot. As an added bonus, B-roll of her frolicking with cows near her Pennsylvania home made her look like a total cowgirl. To say Sabrina was robbed when she came in third in the contest is an understatement.

"That whole experience was interesting. I think that was the first time I really maybe got out of my shell and started to perform in front of the camera," she told *Cosmopolitan*. The execs at Disney noticed that cocooning too, keeping tabs on the budding star in the ensuing years after the contest wrapped and eventually signing her in 2013 to their Hollywood Records label.

As another consolation prize, Sabrina got to meet her idol Miley at a show in Philadelphia. "She told me I was doing awesome," young Sabrina told her local paper *The Morning Call*, admitting she was "starstruck" as Miley autographed her backstage pass. When the reporter asked Sabrina what her long-term goal was, she said, "Hopefully someday, maybe at a little girl's birthday party, they'll have my music on. That would just be an awesome feeling." Sabrina, the lovable tortoise, was already keeping a glass-half-full attitude at that young age.

Even when she lost the MileyWorld Superstar contest, there was no thought of giving up. Instead, her dad built a recording booth in the family home—painted bright purple, her favorite color at the time. It's here that Sabrina would continue to cut vocal takes. "That's where I really found comfort in a creative space," she told *Marie Claire*.

In a real estate listing for the former Carpenter family property in Pennsylvania, the write-up touts a "soundproofed in-law suite," perhaps where those primitive recordings might've taken place. Likely it was the spot where she recorded a song called "Catch My Breath," a single she self-released on iTunes in 2010 with an accompanying low-budget music video.

Sabrina appearing at Gucci Osteria da Massimo Bottura in Beverly Hills, California, in honor of Miley Cyrus's album *Endless Summer Vacation*, March 9, 2023.

What Are the Chances of a Miley Collaboration?

Sabrina is a big fan of combining forces—in her career thus far, she's worked with Charlie Puth, Christina Aguilera, Sofia Carson, Amy Allen, and Jack Antonoff (not to mention Barry Keoghan and Jenna Ortega in music videos). So, could a possible cosign with Miley Cyrus come next? The idea has come up before. When Sabrina was asked in an interview about possibly working with her once hero, she gushed, "I mean, that's my childhood poster girl. I LOVE Miley."

As far as Miley goes, she's had nothing but praise for Sabrina, as well as Olivia Rodrigo and Chappell Roan (all of whom have called the "Flowers" singer an inspiration). Chatting with Spotify's *Billions Club: The Series* in November 2024, Miley said, "You never think about in the future, someone replicating what you do... Now, to see that impacting culture—it's something I didn't know I wanted, but I guess I do." She added, "The freedom I've kind of given these other artists to be themselves, [to] do it proud and loud—it's just amazing to watch that be so impactful and influential."

Miley Cyrus and Sabrina Carpenter at the 67th Annual Grammy Awards, February 2, 2025.

Becoming a Character

Not long after "Catch My Breath" was released, Sabrina landed her first true acting gig in 2011 on an episode of the NBC cult classic series *Law & Order: SVU*. It was her second audition ever. "I got a manager—the same one I have now—and he was very realistic," she shared with *Variety* about her initial career jump. "He said, 'We'll send you out for things—no promise that they're even going to see your tape.' But then, not to brag, I booked one of the first things I ever went for."

In the *SVU* episode called "Possessed," Sabrina plays a young victim named Paula who is wrapped up in a child trafficking ring and helps Agent Stabler break the case open. It wasn't exactly the lighthearted country line dancing of "Hoedown Throwdown," but Sabrina loved it. She told *Teen Vogue* that the role "made me fall in love with acting."

By 2013, she landed on another dark drama, Netflix's *Orange Is the New Black*, playing her first "mean girl," Jessica Wedge. In a throwback scene, Jessica ridicules a young Alex Vause for dressing in "bum's clothes" and for the fact that her mom works at Payless. "It's so hard to watch because I was such a little meanie . . . but what I thought when I was younger was that it would be so fun to play a villain or a mean girl because I was

> *"What I thought when I was younger was that it would be so fun to play a villain or a mean girl because I was like, it's the opposite of me."*

like, it's the opposite of me," she told *Cosmopolitan*. Plus, the episode she appeared on was one called "[F]sgiving," and we all know how much Sabrina loves a good four-letter word.

"I was thrown off by [the *SVU*] booking because I always wanted to do comedy. And on that show, I was a victim. I remember running the lines with my dad and asking, 'Is this what acting is?' And then I booked *Orange Is the New Black* [and wondered] can I swear?" she recalled to *W* magazine. It was a total backward gateway into the more wholesome roles that would come next.

After some voiceover work on the animated series *Phineas and Ferb* in 2012 and appearing in a long-arc role on FOX sitcom *The Goodwin Games* in 2013 (a *Hunger Games*/*Squid Game*–style escapade in which three siblings enter into a series of competitions to win their late father's fortune), soon came a slew of opportunities with Sabrina's long-time dream job, the Disney Channel.

First up was a one-off on the series *Austin & Ally* in 2013, in which Sabrina takes on the art-imitating-life character Lucy Gluckman, a contestant on a fictional singing competition show called *America's Top Talent*. That same year, Sabrina signed on for regular voiceover work on two Disney animated series, *Sofia the First* and *Wander Over Yonder*, before the ultimate gig presented itself: the role of Maya Hart on *Girl Meets World*.

By now, Sabrina had fully moved to Los Angeles so that she could focus on all of these new opportunities, which kept pouring in. "LA won't be getting rid of me just yet!!" she wrote in a Facebook post in 2012, sharing news of being cast for *The Goodwin Games*. The permanency in Hollywood also allowed her to be on set daily for *Girl Meets World*, which was filmed largely at Los Angeles Center Studios five days a week—three days of rehearsing and two days on camera. It was a schedule that introduced Sabrina to the grind of an entertainer. But she's a Taurus after all, and Tauruses love to work. "It's nine-and-a-half hours every day of pure work/fun," Sabrina told Disney Channel Australia & New Zealand during an on-set visit in 2015.

The series (which debuted in 2014 and wrapped production in 2017) was a modern-day follow-up to the popular '90s hit *Boy Meets World*, a show that Sabrina had watched every day before school. "It was my go-to in the morning," she told the *Chicks in the Office* podcast in 2020. "It was a show that I always remembered just loving."

In the sequel, now grown-up Cory Matthews is married to Topanga Lawrence, and their sweet daughter Riley becomes chummy with the hard-edged Maya, who helps Riley navigate some of the crash courses of life.

Sabrina and actress Rowan Blanchard in a scene from *Girl Meets World*.

Sabrina Meets World

During her stint as Maya Hart, it was also a coming-of-age time for Sabrina herself. She played the character from ages fourteen to eighteen and took away a lot of lessons from the experience. "In the moment, that was my world, and that was my everything, and I was so proud to be a part of it and everything that it stood for," Sabrina told *Teen Vogue* in 2020. "I think the beauty of the show was that we really were at the age that we were playing, and we were coming into ourselves."

Because the cast was largely made up of young children, it was also a return to a more traditional school setup for Sabrina, as she and the other actors studied together. "A lot of our most fun times were spent in our classroom," Sabrina shared with *HollyWire*.

She also literally grew during her time on the show. Throughout the filming of *Girl Meets World*, Sabrina measured in at four feet (1.2 m) and ten or eleven inches (25 or 28 cm) but got that last boost by the time the show wrapped in 2017. As she told *WIRED*, "I remember when I hit five foot, I was like doing the Macy's Thanksgiving Day Parade and I found out that day. I measured myself and I was like, did that happen? And I don't think I've grown since."

> *"I remember when I hit five foot, I was like doing the Macy's Thanksgiving Day Parade and I found out that day. I measured myself and I was like, did that happen? And I don't think I've grown since."*

In a 2013 announcement of Sabrina's casting in the Disney series, *The Hollywood Reporter* shared the background of the character Maya Hart, explaining she's "an only child and has never known her father, which makes her relationship with both Riley and Cory Matthews very important to her. She is a wonderful student of life and absolutely magnetic in attracting the people in her sphere. A little bit edgy, she is as fiercely loyal to Riley as Riley is to her."

That kinship between Riley (played by Rowan Blanchard) and Maya was the key to the success of the series and also spilled over into reality as Sabrina and Rowan became fast friends, leading to the advent of Rowbrina. Though they haven't been seen together in public (or on socials) for many years, they were self-admitted besties back then. Sabrina shared a bit about their early bond with *HollyWire* as *Girl Meets World* wrapped production: "We went through like puberty together, which means there's a lot of weird inside jokes."

Back then, not only did the two harmonize together on *Girl Meets World*'s theme song, "Take on the World," but Sabrina also wrote her heartfelt track "Seamless" about her ride or die Rowan. The song appeared on Sabrina's debut album *Eyes Wide Open*, released in 2015 via Disney's Hollywood Records. The label signed Sabrina to its roster when she was just fourteen years old and released her first EP, *Can't Blame a Girl for Trying*, in 2014. The label would go on to support three additional full-length albums, including 2016's *EVOLution*, 2018's *Singular: Act I,* and 2019's *Singular: Act II*. Once the pop star hit twenty, she parted ways with the label to branch out into more adult terrain.

Although the chicken-and-egg order of things seemed like the Disney acting career led to the record deal, Sabrina has been keen on reminding everyone that she was always a musician first and foremost. When *Billboard* published an editorial celebrating Sabrina's rise to No. 43 for *Eyes Wide Open* on the 200 album chart, Sabrina chided them for getting the actor-turned-recording artist verbiage wrong. "If only they knew I was a recording artist turned actor," she posted on Instagram.

She confirmed in her Stars in Cars interview that "music came first. Acting was never something I really knew how to do." In fact, she said she never took official acting classes other than summer camps and after-school theater programs. "It was like finding a new passion . . . But singing was something I never had to question, and writing [music] was something I never had to question. I always knew I loved it." And soon, she'd fall head over foot for it all over again. After *Girl Meets World* was canceled in 2017, Sabrina recalled to *Marie Claire*, "I was just about to turn eighteen, and I was really excited about moving on to the next thing." Everyone, please welcome Sabrina to the stage.

Sabrina promotes *Eyes Wide Open* and *Girl Meets World* at Planet Hollywood Times Square in New York City, June 7, 2015.

FOLLOWING
Sabrina performs at the Disney Channel's Radio Disney Music Awards at the Nokia Theatre in Los Angeles, April 26, 2015.

"Singing was something I never had to question, and writing [music] was something I never had to question. I always knew I loved it."

An Extra Shot

A Carpenter Crossover

While Sabrina hasn't had her *Simpsons* cameo just yet, it may be coming in the future, especially if her aunt Nancy Cartwright has anything to do with it. Nancy, the long-time voice behind the iconic character Bart Simpson, is actually David Carpenter's sister. "Isn't that amazing? Maybe you've known me for a little while, doing this little ten-year-old boy for thirty-five-some years—and some of you guys for way less than that—and find out that I'm related to this superstar. She's pretty amazing," Nancy shared in a July 2024 TikTok video in which she answered fan questions.

Entertainment Weekly reported that Nancy has been a long-time supporter of her niece's career and first posted a video of Sabrina in concert at the Los Angeles, California club The Roxy Theatre back in 2016. The voice actor has gone on to espouse the talents of her niece in recent interviews. When Nancy appeared on *Good Morning America* in December 2024 to promote a holiday episode of *The Simpsons*, Nancy predicted that not only would Sabrina take home Grammys, but she would also be an EGOT winner someday—that holy grail collection of Emmy, Grammy, Oscar, and Tony awards. "She knew at age six . . . that she wanted to work for Disney," Nancy told the morning show, adding, "She has created her own path."

Sabrina has also talked about her famous aunt in the press. In a radio interview in 2021, she said, "I will just say that my whole life, that was the coolest thing in the world to me. I wasn't even allowed to watch the show until I was a bit older . . . the woman is a woman of many talents. She's not just Bart, and she always blows me away." She also told *WIRED* that even though they work in different entertainment fields, "I've learned so much just from observing her."

Actress Nancy Cartwright attends the unveiling of Bart Simpson's "Bartman" sculpture at USC School of Cinematic Arts in Los Angeles, May 8, 2015.

Fans have been all about the Bart–Sabrina connection, too. Some have pleaded with Nancy to have Bart sing "Espresso" on a future episode while another on TikTok commented on the family "resemblance." "Why does Sabrina being related to Bart Simpson make so much sense? It really is a family attitude."

PART 2

EVOLUTION

"I guess my songs are like my timeline and that's really how I decipher who I was as a person then and who I am now."

What's in an album name? For Sabrina, everything. If you read closely between the lines of her six record titles, you'll collect all the Easter eggs to know exactly what she was thinking, feeling, absorbing, and becoming in each era. "I guess my songs are like my timeline and that's really how I decipher who I was as a person then and who I am now," she shared on the *Zach Sang Show* in 2018.

If her eyes were *wide open* and eager to the idea of becoming a pop star in 2015, she certainly was *evolving* just a year later by popping any bubblegum sound on her sophomore album, and becoming even more saucy in the *Emails* and *Short n' Sweet* zingers that would come years later.

"It's all about moments," Sabrina told Apple Music in 2024, regarding her philosophy on the transitional nature of making music, particularly the metamorphosis from her early works to her more adult-themed opuses. "I'm not the same person when I wrote those." But really, who would be between the ages of thirteen and twenty-five?

When *Eyes Wide Open* was written over the course of 2013 and 2014, and then released on April 14, 2015, Sabrina was barely initiated as a teenager and had just started to discover her early thoughts on friendship, love, and life. In a press release for the debut album, the thematic string tying

PREVIOUS
Sabrina attends the Nickelodeon Kids' Choice Awards at Barker Hangar in Santa Monica, California, April 9, 2022.

it all together was described as a journey of "finding one's way in this world"—yet at an appropriate pace. "In a time when everyone is so eager to grow up, Carpenter cowrote songs about appreciating the present moment," the press release added.

You can hear that cherubic nature in the super saccharine songs "Right Now," "Seamless," and "We'll Be The Stars." You can see the innocence in the grandpa cardigan she wears for the cover art accompanying the latter single, or in the demure peasant top for the cover of the *Can't Blame a Girl for Trying* EP. It would be a bit before Sabrina got in on Victoria's Secret.

Eyes Wide Open included all four songs from the previously released EP plus eight new tracks, with a mix of teen pop, soft ballads, a bit of ukulele-driven Hawaiian folk, and some of Sabrina's beloved country. Many noted hints of twang on that early album. Even today, producer Jack Antonoff has (lovingly) compared Sabrina's unique pitch and syncopation to a kind of yodeling. "While Pennsylvania isn't really the country, I can understand how the twangy notes come out in some of my songs," Sabrina told hometown paper *Lehigh Valley Live* in 2015.

Sabrina has been forthcoming with her love of the country genre, often talking about her worship of Dolly Parton, Carrie Underwood, and Taylor Swift. At her Outside Lands performance in 2024, Sabrina invited Kacey Musgraves to duet with her on a Nancy Sinatra cover. A few months later, in the NPR *Tiny Desk* concert, she went full-on rodeo for a down-home take on "Slim Pickins."

In addition to a wide palette of sounds, though, *Eyes Wide Open* also covers a range of topics. While "Right Now" and "Seamless" are, respectively, about living day by day and an ode to her then-bestie Rowan Blanchard, "We'll Be The Stars" was inspired by an outside source: a popular John Green novel and a 2014 movie adaptation from—of course—Disney.

"I had read *The Fault in Our Stars*—it's still one of my favorite books—and when I heard it, that's what I instantly thought of in my head," Sabrina said regarding the message of the song and, really, the whole album, which circles around the idiom that the sky's the limit. As Sabrina noted in the press release, "The one message that I want fans to take away . . . is to never give up no matter what, keep pursuing your dreams. That's how I made the album."

Eyes Wide Open also has maturing feelings of love and lust in "Two Young Hearts." And later in the album, "Too Young" showcases Sabrina fighting back against the idea she couldn't possibly understand love at her age.

"Everybody always tells me that I'm too young to do this, too young to do that, so I wanted to write a song about that," Sabrina shared in an archived behind-the-scenes interview on her official YouTube page. "The one thing everybody can universally relate to at a point in their life is love."

> "The one message that I want fans to take away . . . is to never give up no matter what, keep pursuing your dreams. That's how I made the album."

All About That Cowriter

Luckily, Sabrina did have help from some older and wiser songwriters who already had their hearts torn wide open and guided her on tapping into those emotions. Sabrina has long thrived on the collaborative nature of songwriting teams, and on her EP and *Eyes Wide Open*, she began working with a series of cowriters, most notably Meghan Trainor.

In 2014, Meghan was also beginning her own ascent as a pop star with her viral song, "All About That Bass," which came after years of busting out hit after hit for other stars; among them are J. Lo, Rascal Flatts, and Fifth Harmony. For Sabrina's debut album, Meghan contributed "Can't Blame a Girl for Trying" and "Darling I'm a Mess."

"A lot of people don't know that I wrote Sabrina Carpenter's first song for Disney. It was so cute," Meghan shared in a 2024 appearance on Paris Hilton's *I am Paris* podcast. "I love those memories I get to have now, and I get to see superstars like her blow up and be like, 'I had a song with her once.' It's the biggest honor."

Sabrina also took away much from the experience. "I learned from each different songwriter that I worked with, different techniques and just growing more and more in my voice and my strength and my confidence in myself," she shared in the behind-the-scenes interview on her

YouTube page. "It was really cool to see the transition from when I had my first writing session to my last writing session for the album."

Although Sabrina and Meghan are way overdue for another collab, they haven't done much together since the *Eyes Wide Open* era. (Unless you count Sabrina tackling Meghan's "Like I'm Gonna Lose You" for her popular series of YouTube covers.) But back then, they were pretty tight, with the execs at Disney tagging in Meghan as Sabrina's wingwoman for fame via a series of promotional bits.

In one video, Sabrina and Meghan play a game of "Cell and Tell" with Radio Disney in which they reveal the juiciest messages, most popular emojis, and last calls on their cell phones. None of it was that revealing, to be honest, but when they were asked about the last thing they looked up on the internet, Sabrina—in her trademark candor—shared, "That's terrible, you should never ask people that."

In another promo, the two singers, wearing animal-print onesies, are seen hanging out on a couch with a bowl of popcorn between them. But all of it was a ruse for Sabrina to surprise Meghan with the news that she'd been nominated for a 2016 Radio Disney Music Award (RDMA). Meghan did win her RDMA that year, but so did Sabrina, taking home the award for Best Anthem for the title track on *Eyes Wide Open*. It was actually Sabrina's second RDMA; she was first honored in 2015 for Best Crush Song for "Can't Blame a Girl for Trying."

"I was so, so excited, I didn't know what to say at that moment," she shared in a 2018 Radio Disney throwback about receiving her very first award. "All I know is that year I was in the same category as Nick Jonas, and that's what I said during my speech because I literally just voted for him. I was very confused as to why I won."

It's a Small World, After All

The Disney awards kept coming as Sabrina continued working with Hollywood Records. In 2017 and 2018, she was respectively nominated for RDMA's Best Crush Song for "On Purpose" and one-off single "Why." As a popular Disney star, it was almost a guaranteed fate. Sabrina was just following in the well-paved footsteps of her childhood idols Miley Cyrus and Christina Aguilera, plus Selena Gomez, Demi Lovato, the Jonas Brothers, and Hilary Duff.

For years, the Disney Channel has been a natural pipeline for Top 40 stars. And they have the perfect vehicle for it with Hollywood Records. According to Discogs, the label was "originally created as a way for Disney to distance itself from the 'Disney' brand, and allow more mature music material to be released, similar to what Touchstone Pictures did for Disney's film market." Established in 1990, the first act Hollywood Records signed to the roster was the quintet known as The Party, aka Positive Attitude Reflects Today's Youth, which featured members of *The All-New Mickey Mouse Club*.

Along the way, Hollywood Records also veered off into other territories. One of its biggest gets was nabbing the rights to the catalog of British rockers Queen. That's until Hilary Duff entered the picture. When her 2003 album *Metamorphosis* was released via Hollywood, it became one of its biggest movers and shakers to date on the label with three million copies sold. Naturally, Hollywood saw the momentum and picked up speed in pushing through the Disney actor-musician talent pool, which would include Sabrina a decade later. It was a win–win, if not also a monopoly, that paid off in dividends for everyone. With its multipronged approach across TV, music, and radio, Disney had a massive platform for making bona fide stars with a built-in way to market them across the full entertainment spectrum. Plus, the fact that most Disney stars are children—for better or worse—also made the kids (and their parents) rather pliable and adaptable to the company's goals.

"The main reason why Disney can find hidden gems and propel them into fame is because of the way the company teaches them how the business works," said *Marist Circle*. "Hollywood is fickle, and it certainly isn't a meritocracy, so one has to try and find success not off of their merits, but by their knowledge and understanding of the industry that they're trying to get into. Disney is a perfect place to do that," the outlet added. "These people learn about the business and the inner-workings of fame, success, and especially marketing, as children . . . They learned about Hollywood, fame, money, success, and how to advocate for and market themselves at an age when they were too naive to be cynical. That's the best way to try and understand Disney's impact on these young stars."

Sabrina reaped many of these benefits early on with *Eyes Wide Open* and its four popular music videos, including that memorable sanguine piece for "Can't Blame a Girl for Trying" where she roller-skates around an apartment and quickly changes hats and instruments with some screen magic. "This video lives in a lot of young girls' heads rent-free and I feel very happy and grateful for that," Sabrina told *Cosmopolitan* in a 2024 video interview, while also hiding behind a slight snarl and eye-wincing pain as she rewatched it. "We all have to have that thing we look back on and go like, 'Well, I was young and a lot of choices were made in that video because I was young.'"

Eyes Wide Open placed at No. 43 on the *Billboard* 200 chart in May 2015 and stayed on the chart for four weeks. In the same period, it was also No. 31 on the Top Album Sales chart—which is not bad for a debut. "Is Sabrina Carpenter the Next Selena Gomez?" read a headline in *Vogue* in 2016. Not long after, *Billboard* penned an editorial that posited, "Carpenter has long been primed to become the leader of Disney's next wave of young pop stars." The excitement continued building when *Marie Claire* heralded her a "Gen-Z icon in the making."

Evolution, or Revolution?

To capitalize on the momentum, Sabrina and her team wasted no time in getting out a new single "Smoke and Fire," followed by her sophomore album, *EVOLution*, released on October 14, 2016. As Sabrina was still working heavily—five days a week—on *Girl Meets World*, it meant touring would have to wait, so to fill her time and her catalog, she worked on new music while on set or during any downtime. "Wrote 'Run and Hide' in a hotel room, recorded the demo in one take, that's how it lives on," she shared on X (formerly known as Twitter) of one of the new ballads.

"I love constantly writing music," Sabrina told *Billboard* of the quick turnaround between albums, "and the second I write it, obviously, I want to release it. But it's not as simple as that." She's also compared the need to be prolific to symbolically wanting to feed fans' hunger. "I was talking to my friend how, online, these kids think of it as like, a mother feeding her children. And I'm like, 'I'll keep feeding my children if that's the case. I won't let my kids starve!'"

While a quick year went by between her first two albums, you wouldn't have guessed it by hearing or seeing Sabrina's own massive evolution as she grew up before our eyes and ears in the process. Gone was the teen pop innocence of "Right Now," and in its place was the cabaret scat of "Thumbs." Similarly, the plucky campfire burner "The Middle of Starting

Over" was traded in for the elevated electricity of "On Purpose." On many tracks, her high soprano register is also balanced by her husky chest voice. On the whole, *EVOLution* is a more sophisticated synth-pop effort with R&B instincts that fit in with the milieu of big album launches that same year, like Rihanna's *Anti* and The 1975's *I Like It When You Sleep, for You Are So Beautiful yet So Unaware of It*.

When Sabrina was asked by iHeartRadio about how much the music has changed between the first two albums, she responded, "As much as I've changed from sixteen to seventeen, which is a lot. For all the teenagers that can relate, these are the years where we experience a lot of different feelings and emotions, and I'm just learning that I can write about mine."

In fact, one of the biggest changes that came with *EVOLution* was that Sabrina cowrote every single song except for one ("Thumbs"), versus the four she cowrote on *Eyes Wide Open*. It's a strong sticking point for Sabrina since one of the biggest misconceptions people have long had about her, as she told *CBS News Sunday Morning*, is that "I don't write my music... I think a lot of people think because I have a producer and cowriters that I love that I'm sitting in the room on my phone not writing songs." But that couldn't be further from the truth; in fact, her writing began with the very seeds of her career when she was just ten and wrote her very first song, "I Want To Be In The Lights," even if she still believes it's the worst thing she's ever penned.

"I wanted to know the story behind each and every thing that I was saying," she told iHeartRadio about why owning the songwriting was so important to her on *EVOLution*. "I wanted it to be honest and I wanted it to relate to people, and I wanted it to relate to me because, in the end, I'm singing these songs until I'm sick of them, and I want to love every bit of them."

Like her previous albums, *EVOLution* continued Sabrina's go-to fodder of love and relationships (*EVOL* is love spelled backward, after all), but this time, the serenades were styled in new and distinct ways. There's the jazzy pleading of a paramour in "Feels Like Loneliness" and the R&B fervor of "No Words," which describes the ups and downs of a relationship, plus the tender, whispering album outro, "All We Have Is Love," filled by a background choir of voices.

"On Purpose" and "Thumbs" were both released as singles from the album, with the latter leading to some career firsts for Sabrina; namely, her late-night debut on *The Late Late Show with James Corden* in April 2017, where she performed the song to an audience full of screaming fans. "Thumbs" was also a hit at Top 40 radio, and thus, became her first certified song by the Recording Industry Association of America® (RIAA®), going gold in August 2017 and platinum by November 2020. Overall, *EVOLution* placed at No. 28 on the *Billboard* 200 chart, found traction overseas (particularly New Zealand where it came in at No. 4 on the country's Heatseekers Albums chart), and led to Sabrina's very first headlining tour and some additional key performances.

In a total full-circle moment, Sabrina headlined her first festival ever, years before making her debuts at Coachella, Governors Ball, and Outside Lands. Back in 2016, Sabrina made a bold entrance at MusikFest, held in Bethlehem, Pennsylvania, not far from where she grew up. "That was my first [moment of] like maybe I'm going to be successful," she shared in her *Hot Ones* interview in 2024. "That was such a [big] part of my childhood, going every year, that when I got to headline it, [it] was like this is one of my biggest dreams . . . It's such a gift to watch things and then find yourself getting to do them and you can kind of look back."

Sabrina's hometown papers were there to capture the moment. "The seventy-minute, sixteen-song set was upbeat, professional and energetic and received with cheers, applause, and chants of 'Sabrina, Sabrina' from her mostly school-age fans," said *The Morning Call*, adding it was a "smooth, polished set of buoyant pop accented by her big, belty voice." *Lehigh Valley Live* honed in on the show's greater impact on the impressionable audience. "Kudos for artists like Carpenter for getting young people excited about music," the paper shared.

"I wanted to know the story behind each and every thing that I was saying. I wanted it to be honest and I wanted it to relate to people and I wanted it to relate to me because, in the end, I'm singing these songs until I'm sick of them and I want to love every bit of them."

Becoming Socially Conscious

It would be two more years before Sabrina released her next albums, *Singular: Act I* on November 9, 2018, and its companion piece, *Singular: Act II* on July 19, 2019. But even so, Sabrina's star wattage was growing exponentially over the course of this time, spurred by two dovetailing events. One was her ongoing acting work, which kept her name and face front and center with key demographics. *Girl Meets World* was in its final seasons, which meant that her schedule was starting to open up for new roles. She landed sizable gigs in two movies: Disney's remake of the '80s flick *Adventures in Babysitting* in 2016 as well as the 20th Century Fox film, *The Hate U Give* in 2018, adapted from a novel by Angie Thomas that centered around heavy conversations of police brutality and racism.

The other key development for Sabrina was an uptick in social media sharing that made fans feel even more connected to her—a practice she continues to this day. "I want to do a live chat. I want to see what people are saying," Sabrina told *Marie Claire* of the motivation to have more of an online presence. Through the medium, she was able to increasingly build her fanbase; by 2019, she already had seventeen million followers on Instagram.

Sabrina appearing at the Y100 Jingle Ball at BB&T Center in Sunrise, Florida, December 17, 2017.

EVOLUTION

But social media also gave Sabrina her first real sense of backlash, particularly with the engrossing conversations around *The Hate U Give*. Sabrina's portrayal of affluent white prep school student, Hailey, who was a best-friend-turned-foe of the movie's main character, a Black teen named Starr, set off a firestorm online. As *Marie Claire* reported, "Carpenter had to field Twitter [now known as X] comments from fans like 'Your acting was amazing, but Hailey really got on my nerves tonight' and 'You played a great racist.'" For Sabrina, she told the magazine, "I was just waiting for a project that would stop me in my tracks, and that was it."

Born in 1999, Sabrina's generation was one of the first launched into the era of social media without a real choice in the matter. There was pressure to consistently engage, especially in her fame incubation period—and she read all the mean tweets, even as a young child, when snarky comments were first posted on her YouTube page. But she's also never shied away from it; rather, she's said "bring it on."

"I'm not going to be one of those artists who's going to shut myself off from reading every little thing about me. I'd rather know and accept it . . . than pretend it's not there," she told Apple Music. And even when that decision has proved incredibly difficult—like the literal threats she

> "I'm not going to be one of those artists who's going to shut myself off from reading every little thing about me. I'd rather know and accept it . . . than pretend it's not there."

got during the Olivia Rodrigo–Joshua Bassett scandal—Sabrina has used the chatter as fuel for her music, and in the process, has found her own lane as an artist.

"It's not what I signed up for, but I can't really help when I was born," she told *The Guardian*. "I want to be honest—I want to just write about what's happening in my life as a twenty-five-year-old girl. But it comes with the territory and I just have to be like . . . OK!"

FOLLOWING
Sabrina attends the Nina Ricci show as part of Paris Fashion Week, March 2, 2018.

"I want to be honest— I want to just write about what's happening in my life as a twenty-five-year-old girl."

An Extra Shot

Because She Liked a Boy

Since childhood, Sabrina's true one and only has been music, but she's also found a way to let in some romance on the side.

Sabrina's first rumored paramour was Disney bedfellow Bradley Steven Perry, whom she was linked with in 2014. According to *Elle*, Bradley made one big romantic gesture to ask her out the first time. "[It was] like the pirate movies . . . [with] the little bottles and they put notes in them and send them across the ocean, like one of those, and [he] put a note inside." It's the kind of storyline of a teenage rom-com, one that Sabrina might have otherwise played on screen if it wasn't her real life.

But it's these two—Joshua Bassett and Shawn Mendes—that turned up a few eyebrows, in particular those of Olivia Rodrigo and Camila Cabello. When Sabrina started dating Joshua (another Disney chum) in 2020, let the record state he was in fact single after splitting with Olivia. But Olivia did purportedly take a sly stab at Sabrina in her song "Driver's License," talking about "the blonde" her guy was spending a little too much time with.

As photos of Sabrina and Joshua started making the rounds, fans put two-and-two together and then started coming for Sabrina with intense online backlash and verbal harassment. Sabrina has never talked much about it, but she did coyly share her side in the *Emails I Can't Send* song "Skin." The kicker? Telling the "Driver's License" singer not to "drive herself crazy."

Barry Keoghan and Sabrina Carpenter attend the 2024 Vanity Fair Oscar Party in Beverly Hills, California, March 10, 2024.

Shawn was an even shorter-lived fling in early 2023, and not nearly as dramatic, but it did involve yet another third party. Sabrina and Shawn split as quickly as they got started and then he resumed his back-and-forth relationship with Camila. Fans have been quick to pounce on the fact that the *Short n' Sweet* song "Taste" is about the tryst since Sabrina talks about being back with an ex in the chorus. Others believe there may be some tell-all comments in "Coincidence," "Sharpest Tool," and "Dumb & Poetic."

That's the charm of Sabrina—she's not one to kiss-and-tell, but she will spill the tea in a song and get the ultimate revenge by making it a hit. Her latest romance saga was with Irish actor Barry Keoghan (of *Saltburn*) whom Sabrina was linked with throughout 2024, before the two split in December of that year. "They are both young and career-focused, so they've decided to take a break," a source told *People*. But was there more to it than that? When Barry starred in Sabrina's "Please Please Please" music video in June 2024, many got the confirmation they needed that Sabrina's song—begging her boyfriend not to embarrass her—was indeed about him. She told *The Guardian* that working with him on the video was "one of the best experiences I've ever had. I'm very honored and I got to work with such a great actor." But the article added she then "mock[ed] her own coy diplomacy in a nasal voice" and sarcastically retorted, *"Such a great actor!"*

A Singular Vision

Sabrina started tackling more realism and openness in her *Singular* phase, a pair of companion albums that she called her most personal albums up to that point, and also her first where she cowrote *every single* song. "[I'm] trying to tell the story of a single voice. And not just because I'm single, I just mean the voice alone. It's just one voice . . . whatever," she told Zach Sang, adding, "I was having a conversation with someone that had heard the album and they said it was 'singularly Sabrina' . . . it made me think about the reason behind why so many songs on this album represented this confidence . . . and themes of empowerment . . . things I had to go through on this album to prove that I didn't need certain other people to help me get there."

The first installment in 2018, the dance-pop-heavy *Singular: Act I*, came after a very lucrative two-year writing process and also after guesting with Jonas Blue on the huge club hit "Alien." *Singular: Act I* kicked off with the song "Almost Love," which Sabrina cowrote with Stargate, a Norwegian troupe that had previously written bangers for Beyoncé and Rihanna. She also worked with other additional big wig producers on the album, like Oak Felder and The Orphanage (who had been behind Demi Lovato's hits), and Johan Carlsson, who previously worked with Ariana Grande. "Whenever I listened to it, it made me want to physically get up and dance, and I've never had a song like that," Sabrina told *Billboard*

> *"For those that have been following along on the journey, the feedback that I've got on this song is that it's a 'new Sabrina,' which is exactly what I wanted."*

about "Almost Love," adding, "For those that have been following along on the journey, the feedback that I've got on this song is that it's a 'new Sabrina,' which is exactly what I wanted."

In her 2018 chat with the *Zach Sang Show*, Sabrina added that the song produced "this personality I hadn't explored before . . . It felt like a new voice."

Sabrina explored it further on songs like the R&B gem "Hold Tight," a collaboration with soulful rapper Uhmeer (the kin of DJ Jazzy Jeff), as well as the attitude-soaked, self-worth anthem "Diamonds Are Forever," that unveiled her emerging bravado.

There's also the sultry "Paris," a tongue-in-cheek song about Sabrina's long love affair with the city of romance—one that developed long before she crafted "Espresso" at a French creperie. "I thought if I manifested so hard when I wrote that song, I would get to play Paris so soon," she joked with *Billboard*. During a 2018 Radio Disney interview, a fan asked Sabrina where she'd like to tour, to which she reiterated that desire. "I'd probably love to go to France," she told the listener. For *Short n' Sweet*, half of the album was actually written in the European country over the span of an intensive eleven days, which satisfied a lifelong dream for Sabrina. "I've wanted to write in France my whole life . . . I thought, it'll be creatively inspiring, and I was right," she told Apple Music in 2024.

> *"I thought if I manifested so hard when I wrote that song, I would get to play Paris so soon."*

But a true standout from *Singular: Act I* was the song "Sue Me," Sabrina's first true genius clapback. It was her take on veiled "Bye Bye Bye" revenge–whereas *NSYNC took the reins back from their con artist ex-manager, Sabrina was taking aim at her own former business managers, Stan Rogow and Elliot Lurie, who actually did sue her in 2017, alleging she failed to pay them commissions when she fired them four years prior. "It's empowerment. It's confidence. It's being comfortable with yourself regardless of what anybody thinks," Sabrina shared in a performance of the hit on *Live with Kelly & Ryan*.

"Sue Me" was another certified hit, officially labeled a gold single by the RIAA® in 2020; it also reached No. 1 on the Dance Club Songs chart in 2018, which was new territory that Sabrina dominated in this era ("Almost Love" and "Alien" also reached the top of that chart the same year). In total, *Singular: Act I* placed at No. 103 on the *Billboard* 200 chart, a good fifty-plus spots down from the No. 43 spot that *EVOLution* was seated at. *Singular: Act II* fared no better, coming in at No. 138. Whether that was due to the long lag between albums, or the new subject material, is up for debate; but either way, Sabrina wasn't changing course. "Some of the best advice I've gotten is to sing what you know best, and I've always been an avid believer in feeling what you're singing," she once shared in a video on her YouTube page.

Sabrina appearing as the music guest on *The Late Late Show with James Corden*, October 1, 2018.

FOLLOWING
Sabrina onstage at the Y100 Miami Jingle Ball in Sunrise, Florida, December 16, 2018.

"Some of the best advice I've gotten is to sing what you know best, and I've always been an avid believer in feeling what you're singing."

Kids These Days

As Sabrina was growing up, she was also at the appropriate age to start shedding her Disney visage just like Britney, Christina, and Miley had done before—granted, without a lot of the headlines and scrutiny they had once faced. "It's so funny to me that it's become this huge stigma over the years that there has to be a transition," Sabrina told *Clevver News* in 2020. "They put so much pressure on that point from when you're done being on [the] Disney Channel, on a show, to whatever you do next. Honestly, I was just always doing what I loved, and I continue to do what I love and follow the projects and follow the things that my heart kind of tells me to and my heart leads me to."

Sabrina, for the most part, came out unscathed from any kind of perceived child star downfall and only kept ascending to her eventual throne, which was mostly by design. "I think I was born somebody that really wants to control my narrative and knows that in the end, the choices that I make now are choices that will affect me later and [in the] long term," she once told *Teen Vogue*.

But there were those who held out hope for a Disney comeback. When the company announced in 2024 that a live-action version of the movie *Tangled* was coming, fans on socials all but demanded Sabrina be cast as the lead.

"I think I was born somebody that really wants to control my narrative and knows that in the end, the choices that I make now are choices that will affect me later and [in the] long term."

"I'm 900 inappropriate jokes away from being a Disney actor," she joked with *Variety* in an interview that same year. She told *Billboard*, "For a lot of people, their first impression of me was as a thirteen-year-old girl [singing] the kinds of songs that she should be singing. Then, flash forward to nineteen, and people are asking why I am not singing about the same things that I did when I was thirteen, as if that's normal . . . Because of my history, it's always something that I'll have to deal with and get over."

On *Singular: Act II*, Sabrina started and continued exploring the maturing, messy, and non-squeaky-clean side of herself. Her first expletive-laced lyric dropped in this era, though in a song that didn't make it to the *Singular* albums. "The first song that I dropped the f-bomb in, everyone pulled out champagne and they're like you can't have it, but we're going to cheers for you," she joked on the *Zach Sang Show*. "They're just words," she conceded of her favorite vocabulary. "But I'll only do it if I feel like it needs to be there . . . there has to be a meaning and purpose behind it."

Elsewhere on Sabrina's 2019 album, there's the quippy personal track "Pushing 20," a biological clock countdown that masks as a hip-hop hit. Sabrina wrote it in May 2019 on her twentieth birthday. It's such a revelation *Popsugar* included the track in their list of "9 Songs For the

20-Somethings Who Are Living, Loving, and Learning Their Way Into Adulthood." More hip-hop experimentation continues on "I Can't Stop Me," a drill track cowritten with Stargate and featuring rapper Saweetie.

But one of the true attention-grabbers from *Singular: Act II* is the catchy dream pop single "In My Bed." It's about some of the anxiety the up-and-coming star was dealing with at the time that could sometimes sideline her. "It's very hard to define it; it comes in waves," she told *Marie Claire* in 2019. "I have to constantly remind myself that I'm doing what I love and there's so much to be grateful for." Her ruminations on the topic of anxiety, stress, and feeling overwhelmed also come to a head again later in the album, on the beautifully poignant "Exhale."

"I really didn't know if I was ever going to release it. It was intimate and I didn't want it to seem like a moment of like, wanting attention in the wrong way," she told *PopCrush*. "I'm naturally a very confident person but I think it's important to know that even people who are always happy and confident, it's not like that 100 percent of the time. It's always good to check in on those people."

> "I'm naturally a very confident person but I think it's important to know that even people who are always happy and confident, it's not like that 100 percent of the time. It's always good to check in on those people."

Trying to catch her breath became a huge struggle in the latter part of the 2010s as Sabrina was juggling an insurmountable project pile. Even if she's always credited for her incredible "work ethic," she was no robot and trying to manage acting, recording, and touring at the same time would be enough to implode any human. Let alone someone who felt *everything*.

The Reviews Are In...

Sabrina's been a critical darling since the beginning. Here's what journalists had to say about her first four albums:

"*Eyes Wide Open* showcases her heartfelt acoustic pop sound... Carpenter takes a further step into the limelight with a collection of songs that build nicely upon her likable screen persona and knack for delivering charming, melodic tunes."—*AllMusic*

"With *EVOLution*, Sabrina is showing a mature musical side, willing to experiment with techno beats, lyrics, and what she can do vocally. She provides an interesting indie yet synth take on pop music, and has clearly found a unique sound that she shines in, that separates her from the rest."—*ANDPOP.com*

"*Singular: Act I* finally conveys the singer in a space equipped for showcasing her talent and attraction as a pop artist and performer moving to the bigger stage. This latest album shows immense promise for the future of her discography as she continues to cement her place as one of the top new artists in this next generation of musicians."—*EARMILK*

"If 2018's *Singular: Act I* was an introduction to Carpenter's playful psyche, *Singular: Act II* invites listeners to peer inside her head. The singer's fourth studio album is a glossy, hook-laden collection of danceable pop and R&B that explores the twenty-year-old star's intimate perspectives, emotions, and internal musings about everything from love to growing up."—*PopCrush*

Sabrina performs at Highline Ballroom in New York City, November 21, 2016.

A Total Boss Lady

High emotions continued in her moving indie film, *The Short History of the Long Road*, where Sabrina plays Nola, a young girl who lives with her father out of a van, going wherever the wind and road take them, until tragedy strikes and the young girl forges ahead on her own. It was a transformative experience for both the character and the actress. To play the part, Sabrina dyed her hair brown, went without makeup, and didn't even shave for months. "I think this is one of the realest projects I've ever done," she told *Nylon*, and part of it was not really recognizing her own self until she had gone through the whole process. Being Nola helped her realize that her own "innate senses turn on during moments of panic and [seeing] something wrong . . . The way that you react to things; it showed me my initial automatic reflexes, and how strong and quick they are."

In this era, Sabrina also scheduled regular voiceover work for the show *Milo Murphy's Law*, was cast in Disney's musical drama *Clouds*, and soon enough, she took on more lighthearted Netflix films like *Tall Girl* and *Tall Girl 2* (everything truly is always about her height), as well as the thriller *Emergency* for Amazon Prime Video. There was also *Work It* for Netflix, a dance-comedy that put her early choreography training into good practice and aligned with some of her own favorite movies. "I grew up wishing that I was in them and wishing that Channing Tatum was dipping me," she told *Teen Vogue* as one example. *"Dirty Dancing*'s a classic, obviously," she continued. *"Honey*, *Center Stage*, the *Step Up* movies are probably my favorite if I had to choose, especially Moose from *Step Up 2*; my heart belongs to him."

Work It also gave Sabrina her first experience behind the producer chair, making it no coincidence that, around this time, she launched her own company, At Last Productions. Early on, it was attached to a remaking of *Alice in Wonderland* for Netflix, in which she was set to star. The project was announced in 2020, though as of publication, it still hasn't come to fruition. However, At Last was behind her epic *A Nonsense Christmas with Sabrina Carpenter* special for the network.

If work kept her busy, it didn't go unnoticed. In 2020, *Forbes* penned Sabrina on its powerful "30 Under 30" list, noting her "sights are as high" for what she had accomplished and looked to do in the future. *Nylon* also added Sabrina to their list of "25 Gen Z'ers Changing The World." In the article, she shared that she had a bit of inspiration she borrowed from another music artist. "Once, I heard Bruno Mars say he was just getting started—and that was after he had a few grammys under his belt. Ever since then, I realized, if Bruno's still just getting started, then I'll always be just getting started." And that perspective carried her *swiftly* to an opportunity that came just a few years later.

FOLLOWING
Sabrina poses for a portrait during the 2019 Tribeca Film Festival in New York City, April 26, 2019.

EVOLUTION

"I realized, if Bruno [Mars]'s still just getting started, then I'll always be just getting started."

PART 3

PRFCT'ING HER LIVE ACT

In her earliest touring days, Sabrina had a short list of essentials in her rider when she headed out on tour: "Immunity shots so I don't get sick, a lot of peanut M&M's . . . and chocolate-covered espresso beans," she told *HollyWire*. Yes, that's right, she said espresso beans. It would take a bit to upgrade to straight-up "Espresso" on her latest tour, on top of many baby steps Sabrina had to take before she could gracefully cascade down the spiral staircase of her Short n' Sweet Tour Dreamhouse.

Before selling out massive arenas like New York's Madison Square Garden, there were small club gigs like Los Angeles' 2,300-cap room, The Wiltern. And before Sabrina's headliner name was firmly on the marquee, it was in smaller font, underneath megastars like Ariana Grande and Taylor Swift when she performed as their opening acts.

Sabrina's first tour came in late 2016: The forty-two-date EVOLution Tour kicked off that October in Nashville and wrapped up the following May with five dates in Europe that included Sabrina's bucket list destination, Paris. It was quickly followed by the thirty-five-date Summer De-Tour across North America the following July and August. "As soon as I wrapped the third season of [*Girl Meets World*], I went straight into tour, because I hadn't gotten the chance for my first album," she told *Billboard*. "You have to put in the time, and you have to put in the effort in order to have these songs be heard . . . because there is so much music in the world," she added.

Because Sabrina didn't have the chance to cut her teeth with intimate open mics or coffeehouse gigs, or even a real tour before her second album (when she was already becoming a household name), it was a bit

PREVIOUS
Sabrina performing on stage at Melbourne Cricket Ground for Taylor Swift's The Eras Tour, February 16, 2024.

> *"You have to put in the time, and you have to put in the effort in order to have these songs be heard ... because there is so much music in the world."*

of a trial by fire the first time around. "There's no way you can prepare yourself for a tour. There's no class, no online tutorials," she lamented to *Vanity Fair* in 2017. "It's a whirlwind. You're going to cities you haven't been to before, and people are singing your lyrics with you."

Though Sabrina did have some inspiration and know-how from the times she was in the audience herself, like at the very first concerts she attended: Hilary Duff and Kelly Clarkson. "Ever since I was a little girl, when I started to go to concerts, I always take away one thing from each performer that I see," she shared during an *On Air with Ryan Seacrest* interview in 2018. "Even if you're not into their music, you can find something about how they talk to the audience, or how they connect with the audience, or maybe it's how their show is set up and how the show flows. There's always something that I can leave a concert feeling inspired by and then I can use that for future shows like mine."

According to reviews of Sabrina's first tour dates on the EVOLution Tour, it was pretty standard stage fare—but her comfortability was natural from the start. *The Leaf-Chronicle* noted the show had pink and purple stage lights, confetti bombs and rafter streamers, and Sabrina's name in a neon haze behind her on stage. She was also joined by a solid band (including her sister Sarah on backup vocals) and excelled in her accessibility.

By the time Sabrina headed out on her Summer De-Tour later in 2017, the venues had been modestly upgraded to more intimate theaters, and the stage production leveled up, too. "A giant screen displaying mini video clips, photo outtakes, and ambient artwork created a larger atmosphere in addition to the ever-changing lights," said *Music Existence* of the vibe. There were covers in this era, too. At Sabrina's gig in Nashville, she offered Patsy Cline's "Crazy" and Ariana Grande's "Into You." There were also some special guests; at that same show, Sabrina's *Adventures in Babysitting* costar Jet Jurgensmeyer joined to duet on "Can't Blame a Girl for Trying."

Like *Leaf-Chronicle's* review, *Music Existence* also narrowed in on Sabrina's keen ability to connect with her audience, writing, "Carpenter has found her home on stage, interacting with the crowd with confidence and ambition." Her sense of humor was there in the early days, too—at a show in Toronto in 2016, Sabrina pranked her tour openers, Citizen Four, as they covered Nick Jonas' "Bacon" by dressing in the pig meat costume and handing out piping hot strips of the breakfast food to the crowd.

"Ever since I was a little girl, when I started to go to concerts, I always take away one thing from each performer that I see... There's always something that I can leave a concert feeling inspired by and then I can use that for future shows like mine."

Sabrina performing at the iHeartRadio Jingle Ball in Tampa, Florida on December 16, 2017.

Tearing Down Walls

Since the beginning, Sabrina has become incredibly close with her audiences and has only built on that rapport in later years. "I think I really started to realize that I was growing up with my fans when I started touring at sixteen," she told *Cosmopolitan*.

As the blog *You're So Beautiful* explained in a review of a De-Tour stop in New Jersey, "Sabrina has talked a lot this tour about how she wanted to unify people with her art. She spoke about this in person, telling her audience that even if they had nothing else in common with anyone else in the room, they can at least find a bond through their love for music."

Even today, Sabrina comes down from the upper level of her stage penthouse and takes time to talk to people in the front row, whether it's doling out life advice, facilitating proposals, or handcuffing hotties with her pink cuffs. "I like to take people out of the show for a second, it just makes it feel a little bit more like a slumber party," she shared in a *Hot Ones* interview. However, go easy on her if she misses your seat. Sabrina has admitted she can really only see the front row, given the bright lights and stage distance. "When people are like, 'Look for me in the crowd,' I'm like, okay babe, I'll try. I'll do my best," she joked in an interview with *Cosmopolitan*.

There's also a real practicality to these interactions, as she told Apple Music. "Touring for me, I think it's created the space for people to understand that there's a human behind the songs, there's a human behind the music, and there's a human behind the big hair and crazy outfits." Coming up with new "Nonsense" outros every night on the Emails I Can't Send Tour and The Eras Tour, or covering a different song for each stop on the Short n' Sweet Tour, isn't just fun and games, it's also about making the crowd feel special and proving she's no ordinary visitor to their town. "It's like they're your best friends," she told Ryan Seacrest of her typically sold-out audiences. "There's no screen between you and there's no filters. It's just real, which is why I love that concerts are still existing. After all this time and all that's happened with social media, it's still that one thing you can always count on, to go to a concert and see someone in person; you're seeing all their imperfections, you're seeing all their flaws but still you're having a great time . . . It's still a fun thing, that human interaction."

"It's just real, which is why I love that concerts are still existing. After all this time and all that's happened with social media, it's still that one thing you can always count on."

By the time Sabrina embarked on her twenty-one-date Singular Tour in 2019—a jaunt that brought her to Asia for the first time—radio conglomerate Audacy declared, "Everyone needs to see Sabrina Carpenter's high energy, dance-filled set," praising the show's "stadium-level energy, production, and choreography . . . that's leagues ahead of most solo pop stars." Sabrina advanced again on this concert sprawl, donning a dazzling all-gem outfit, bringing on backup dancers in addition to her sizable live band (still including sister Sarah on backup vocals), and adding in more video vignettes. "With grace and talent that parallels arena headliners like Dua Lipa and Ariana Grande," said Audacy, "it's easy to imagine where the 'Almost Love' queen will be in just a few years." How right they were.

Sabrina takes part in the *Good Morning America* Summer Concert Series in New York City, July 5, 2019.

FOLLOWING
Sabrina at the *Billboard* NMPA Grammy Week Songwriter Showcase in Los Angeles, California, February 1, 2023.

"To go to a concert and see someone in person, you're seeing all their imperfections, you're seeing all their flaws but still you're having a great time . . . It's still a fun thing, that human interaction."

Two Five-Foot Pop Princesses

Of course, in the midst of all this, Sabrina had some incredible opportunities opening for other artists, like the British pop/rock band The Vamps as well as the crème de la crème of pop queens—and her personal "girl crushes"—Ariana and Taylor.

"She has some of the most passionate fans in the world and also, in Brazil... they are lovers of music. So I think together it's going to be an incredible show and I'm pretty excited," Sabrina told *HollyWire* ahead of joining Ariana Grande in South America for two dates on her 2017 Dangerous Woman Tour.

The Brazil concerts came just a month after Ariana's UK show was the target of the tragic Manchester Arena Bombing, and the shows marked the star's triumphant return to the stage. "I think she's such a strong and powerful... she's just someone to really look up to after the way she handled it," Sabrina told *Clevver News*, "just fighting evil with love and letting love win. It's the best possible tactic."

When she caught up with Ryan Seacrest a year after the jaunt wrapped, Sabrina talked more about the "incredible" experience she had. "The whole show was beautiful, it celebrates so much love and acceptance, and to be a part of it was just so crazy."

Fans have been pushing for a Sabrina x Ariana collab ever since—and at least one of them is locked into the idea. "I've always been a huge fan," Sabrina told England's Capital FM Radio, noting at the time she had just dug up "this really sad, pathetic tweet where I thought like I discovered Ariana Grande."

That conversation picked up steam again after Ariana's well-timed *Saturday Night Live* spoof in October 2024. As the *Wicked* star hosted the NBC show, one of the sketches featured Ariana leading a pack of bridesmaids and a mysterious "Domingo" in a very off-key riff on "Espresso." Sabrina stood behind it, though, sharing the clip on her Instagram story with the caption, "very nice and on pitch," supported by a pair of heart emojis. "Tysm, we tried," Ariana posted in response.

The skit was so popular that at the SNL50 Anniversary Special, Sabrina, along with a bunch of actors and singers, did a remake in the "Domingo: Vow Renewal" sketch. This time, in a nod to Ariana, Sabrina spoofed the *Wicked* song "Defying Gravity" and even gave that iconic belt note a try, off-key, of course.

FOLLOWING
Sabrina attends the 2022 American Music Awards at Microsoft Theater in Los Angeles, California, November 20, 2022.

Then Came the Emails

Sabrina's newfound catapult into the spotlight as a primetime tour opener was running concurrent with her reinvention as a serious—and seriously sassy—pop star. In 2022, Sabrina released her fifth album, *Emails I Can't Send*, even though in many ways it was also a first. Her first on a new label, Island Records (also the home of Chappell Roan), and the first she considered to be a "big-girl album." As Sabrina told *Variety*, "Island kind of let me run off and make the album I always dreamt of making that I couldn't make before . . . for political reasons I can't get into," she added, alluding to the tenuous relationship with her former home, Hollywood Records.

"I was at a really, really low point in my life about two years ago, so I was writing very few optimistic love songs . . . I just hid and went into this hole of a shelter for a year, and then I was like, 'I'm gonna put it out.'"

Sabrina first signed with Island in 2021, during the COVID-19 pandemic, and came out fully charged with the "Skin" tease. The song debuted at No. 48 on the *Billboard* Hot 100, her first time ever on that chart. As she worked on the full album, it took on an existential life of its own, which spurred her to open up like she had never done before. The album title (like previous monikers) was quite literal, as *Vogue* explained, "Many of the lyrics for the thirteen songs that make up the record actually began with emails that Carpenter would write during the pandemic," but never sent, at least not until the album came out on July 15, 2022. It was three years after *Singular: Act II* and, to date, her longest break between albums. "I took my time with it," she told *Billboard,* then shared with *Vogue* that the process was "a kind of therapy."

Emails I Can't Send came just after Sabrina starred on Broadway as Cady Heron in a very abbreviated run of *Mean Girls* before the pandemic shut everything down. "It humbled me very quickly," she told *CBS News Sunday Morning.* "I was sent home and just was like, 'Wow. I feel like I could do eight shows a week, you know, and I've been training for it and now it's just silence."

Not only was Sabrina isolated in her home at the time, like everyone else trying to keep their distance, but she felt a void that inspired the new material, with much of it taking on a very new tone. "I was at a really, really low point in my life about two years ago, so I was writing very few optimistic love songs," she told *Interview* of that period. "I just hid and went into this hole of a shelter for a year, and then I was like, 'I'm gonna put it out,'" she revealed to *Variety.*

Out of necessity, Sabrina wrote most of the songs solo in the beginning, admittedly inspired by Dolly Parton, Carly Simon, and Carole King. But she soon formed a solid circle of cowriters to help polish the tracks, among them Julia Michaels (the hitmaker behind "Issues"), JP Saxe (who wrote the grammy-nominated "If the World Was Ending" with Julia), Amy Allen (who worked with Harry Styles and Justin Timberlake), and Steph Jones (a collaborator of Florence & The Machine and Teddy Swims). The creative chemistry was so good, *Billboard* said it "helped draw out the pop star's confessional side while understanding how to deploy her more conversational tone." And realizing this winning formula, many of them stuck with her when it came time to write *Short n' Sweet*. "I've really honed in on the people that I love making music with," Sabrina told *Rolling Stone*. "That's the only way those borderline-idiotic-slash-funniest lyrics can happen."

As painful as Sabrina's melancholy was around *Emails*, it actually satisfied an artistic desire—she wanted to feel heartbreak. All of it. "To my friends, I was always like, 'I just want to know what Adele's feeling,'" Sabrina told *Billboard*. "Like, how she made these gut-wrenching records. And I [just became] so fascinated with that . . . like, '[Dang], I just need some of whatever Adele was drinking!' . . . And then I got it."

Sabrina's gut-wrenching heartbreak wasn't her only muse for *Emails I Can't Send*, however; she also ruminated on the fissures in her parents' relationship after finding out her father, David, had an extramarital affair—and some of the songs became her trying to understand how the fallout affected her own ability to love. The gripping title track spills a diary's worth of feelings on the matter. As she told *American Songwriter*, the song "sets this precedent of someone that I love [who] let me down and it changed the way that I view love forever. Now it's in my head. Every time I meet someone or every time I experience a situation, I'm not going into it the way that I did when I was a child when no one hurt me, and when I was trusting and loving and accepting, excited and willing."

FOLLOWING
Sabrina attends Universal Music Group's 2023 Grammy after party in Los Angeles, California, February 5, 2023.

> *"I was always like, 'I just want to know what Adele's feeling.' Like how she made these gut-wrenching records. And I [just became] so fascinated with that."*

"I am a daddy's girl," she added in a chat with *Variety*, saying that the title track was admittedly hard to put out into the world. "It marked the beginning of a really freeing and artistic time for me... My family has just gone through so much that now we're all in a healing stage. As I've gotten older, I've started learning about men and relationships. I'm not perfect by any means, but it definitely makes you look at your parents differently."

That torrent of feelings continues on "Tornado Warnings," where Sabrina rails against a toxic ex, followed by the spoken word poetry of "Skinny Dipping," about running into a past flame at a café and finally getting closure. And of course, there's the revealing "Because I Liked a Boy" that carried on the conversation of the Olivia–Joshua situation and Sabrina's reaction to being put in front of a jury of public opinion that was so convinced she was guilty. "People can say whatever they want to say, but I was lucky to be able to verbalize an experience that some people have been through," she told *Rolling Stone*. "Hopefully it has helped them get through their experience with a little bit more strength and understanding. If I can do that, then I don't have regrets."

"Every time I meet someone or every time I experience a situation, I'm not going into it the way that I did when I was a child when no one hurt me."

The Deep Cuts

For as much as Sabrina opened up on the *Emails I Can't Send* album, it was really the deluxe edition, *Fwd:*, that showed her at her most raw and vulnerable—but not exactly for the track you're thinking of.

While the revenge song "Feather" got all the attention, it's actually companions "Opposite," "Lonesome," and "Things I Wish You Said" that are even more surprising standouts. All three are soft-spoken acoustic ballads mired in melancholy, expressing the very real pain of unrequited love, relationships broken beyond repair, and overwhelming feelings of being alone. It was like few things Sabrina had released in her "big girl" era, but that showed her maturing propensity for coming at heartbreak from two sides of the coin.

Her "jokes on you" pop bangers are fun and empowering, but it's the *Fwd:* sad ballads that are what we need when we just want to go home and cry into a pillow. "Part of me was able to let a lot more walls down because I wasn't confined, like I had been in my previous situation," she told *Variety* of her new record label, Island, giving her the freedom to fully express herself. "I think a lot of my childhood was people telling me what I can and cannot say, or what they think I should be able to say, because I'm supposed to raise their children or something." With *Emails* and the deluxe edition, Sabrina finally quit being the babysitter.

> Sabrina at the Spotify Best New Artist event in West Hollywood, California, February 2, 2023.

A Sick Sense of Humor

Emails I Can't Send was the recipient of unanimous raving reviews, with journalists taking note of the more sophisticated singer who was climbing the ranks of the pop ladder. *The Edge* called it "a piece of art." *The Guardian* exclaimed, "pop's next big thing is best when she lets loose." And *Vogue* said the album represented "the most fully realized vision of Carpenter the musician—and the most rounded portrait of Carpenter the human being—yet." The attention generated a RIAA® gold-certified hit with "Skin" and a double-platinum hit for the deluxe track "Feather." The album as a whole was also certified platinum and peaked at the No. 23 spot on the *Billboard* 200 chart, spending sixty-six weeks in varying positions.

Sabrina wasn't quite done with the album just yet, though. Even after it was released, there was more to explore. "I questioned [*Emails I Can't Send*] until the day it came out: Is it done and could I have changed it? Could I have written another song?" she shared with Apple Music. "To be fair, I do have a hard time with the fact that I do feel like life doesn't stop so it's really hard to tell when a chapter of your life should be bookended . . . other than the fact that you just have a feeling."

> *"To be fair, I do have a hard time with the fact that I do feel like life doesn't stop so it's really hard to tell when a chapter of your life should be bookended... other than the fact that you just have a feeling."*

The deluxe edition of the album, *Emails I Can't Send Fwd:*, was released on March 17, 2023, in the middle of the explosive Emails I Can't Send Tour. Spanning eighty dates and four continents across late 2022 to August 2023, the itinerary included a spread of theaters and amphitheaters across the US, Canada, South America, Europe, and Asia. In *aAh!* magazine's review of the Manchester, England date, they noted the aesthetic, writing, "Sabrina set the scene of a love story with a giant love-heart mirror and a balcony belonging to a fairy-tale."

The tour ended with her much-anticipated Lollapalooza debut in 2023. It was heralded as a "hyper-feminine" affair (*Disrupted* magazine) as the star dazzled in a pink heart-shaped crop top, go-go boots, and rhinestone cowboy hat, with some of her ensemble a subtle nod to Dolly Parton, whom Sabrina said was the angel on her shoulder while making her fifth album.

While the tour included high points of heavy choreography, costuming in the form of corsets and garters, and covers from Shania Twain to Gwen Stefani, the real hero was the unassuming hit "Nonsense," and the litany of viral moments it launched as Sabrina stitched together brand-new, R-rated lyrical passages every night, tailored to each city.

> *"People in the past had told me my music didn't have symmetry, that I didn't have every song sounding the same, and that got in my head. So I'm grateful because the fans decided on their own that it meant something to them."*

"Some people know me for, I guess, being explicitly [sexual]. It's actually not as simple as that," she joked during her NPR Music *Tiny Desk* session. "It's actually a beautiful and happy accident. On my last tour, I started doing these outros as part of a song–these were never lyrics that made it to the end of the song. These were all like reject lyrics and lyrics that honestly should never be heard by the general public. And as a joke I was like well Boston can handle it . . . and Boston handled it so well that I was like well what about Chicago? And then it kind of kept going."

It makes it even more crazy to think that "Nonsense" nearly didn't make the final cut for the album. "That one always stuck out. I felt like it might discredit some of the songs on the album that were about more sensitive subjects, so it almost didn't make it in," she divulged to *Interview*. "People in the past had told me my music didn't have symmetry, that I didn't have every song sounding the same, and that got in my head. So I'm grateful because the fans decided on their own that it meant something to them."

The incredible reaction to "Nonsense" also gave Sabrina faith in her own instincts. "It made me want to trust my personal favorites a little bit more," she told *Hot Ones*. "The lesson I learned with 'Nonsense' was this song was so kindred with my personality and I started to get in my head, like what fits a record versus what fits Sabrina . . . It taught me so many lessons moving forward with making the next record. I think now, whatever feels the most honest and connects to me the most I feel will connect with other people." And that's really the long and short (and sweet) of it, isn't it?

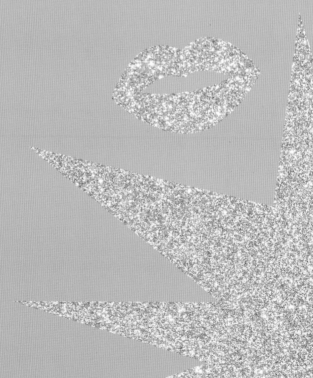

You Belong with Me

The biggest response in Sabrina's inbox after *Emails* was an invitation to join the holy grail of opportunities: The Eras Tour. From August 2023 to March 2024, Sabrina joined Taylor Swift on a jet-setting international sprawl. In November it included stops in Mexico, Argentina, and Brazil. The following February and March, she also tagged along for stops in Australia and Singapore.

By now, we know all the non-hyperbolic achievements of The Eras Tour, like how it broke copious records, such as crossing the two billion-dollar threshold, spawning the highest-grossing concert film of all time, and birthing the "Taylor Swift Effect." But tour openers like Sabrina Carpenter also saw a seismic effect in their careers just from being associated with it. Six months after her final opening slot in Singapore, three of Sabrina's *Short n' Sweet* songs placed in the Top 5 of the *Billboard* Hot 100 in the same exact week–that's a serious Taylor-level feat.

Touring with her fellow Pennsylvanian was a "childhood dream come true," Sabrina told *Who What Wear* in early 2024. "I'm not gonna say I peed my pants because that sounds really graphic and maybe not sanitary, but I think it really just caught me off guard . . . I still probably have not processed it if I'm being completely honest with you." To prepare for the biggest gig of her life up to that point, Sabrina

> "Watching [Taylor] is a masterclass in itself. Obviously, she's very good with words."

told *Rolling Stone* she was going to take cues from the woman of the hour. "Watching [Taylor] is a masterclass in itself. Obviously, she's very good with words. So I feel a lot more comfortable that I'm going into a situation with someone that I admire so much and I'm just gonna like study."

Sabrina was seventeen when she first met Taylor backstage at one of the Anti-Hero's shows. "She had her cats with her," Sabrina recalled to *Who What Wear*. (We can only hope it was her pet Olivia Benson and the two chatted all night about *SVU*.) Sabrina said from that first moment, it felt like a "sister relationship," adding that "to work with someone [who] cares about you as a person as well as an artist . . . that's been the biggest gift for sure."

By 2022, Swiftie Sabrina was hanging out with Taylor at the VMAs and AMAs. In 2023, she was mulling around backstage at several Eras Tour stops before officially getting the opening gig that summer. She also appeared at KC Chiefs games and released a cover of "I Knew You Were Trouble" that Taylor approved, saying Sabrina "nailed it." In 2024, there were day dates to the zoo while on tour in Australia and, when they got back to the States, double dates with their beaus, Travis and Barry. Taylor even promoted *Short n' Sweet* on her social media that August, calling it "an extraordinary album" and declaring it to be the "summer of Sabrina . . . may it continue forever." Taylor then invited Sabrina to *come back* to The Eras Tour for a couple of stops in New Orleans a few months later so they could duet together on a surprise song mash-up of "Espresso," "Please Please Please," and Taylor's "Is It Over Now?"

"She's one of my best, best friends, and we grab dinner or text and catch up like you would with your best friend," Sabrina told *Variety*.

> *"She's one of my best, best friends, and we grab dinner or text and catch up like you would with your best friend."*

By the time the tour wrapped up, Sabrina posted a heartfelt message on Instagram recapping all the extraordinary moments. "Sitting at home reflecting on what a whirlwind this was and how very honored I feel to have been part of it. I want to thank every crowd for being so welcoming and generous to us and making some of the most impressive friendship bracelets I've ever received," she said, "and the most thank you's I've ever thank you'd to Taylor. I feel so lucky to witness the magic that is you and this tour. There is truly no one like you and there never will be! I love you with all my heart and I will cherish this Taybrina era (and all the eras) till the end of time."

With the Taybrina Era coming to its end, a new era of Sabrina was just beginning.

Taylor Swift and Sabrina attend the 2023 MTV Video Music Awards in Newark, New Jersey, September 12, 2023.

FOLLOWING
Taylor Swift and Sabrina attend the 67th Annual Grammy Awards at Crypto.com Arena in Los Angeles, California, February 2, 2025.

"I feel a lot more comfortable that I'm going into a situation with someone that I admire so much and I'm just gonna like study."

An Extra Shot

All Jacked Up

Jack Antonoff knows a pop star when he hears one. From Taylor Swift to Lana Del Rey, Lorde, and now Sabrina, the Bleachers frontman has worked with them all, transforming into an incredibly in-demand producer over the past decade. But lately, it's been all about building Sabrina. "How brilliant is she?" he responded when Grammy.com asked him about his latest ingenue. "It was a big deal for me to get to work with her. The great parallel is brilliant writing … It sounds so simple, but it's the rarest thing to be able to write about your life and to be able to make it so specific and also so poetic."

In a chat with *Rolling Stone*, Jack added that he was immediately drawn to her directness. "I think that the aesthetic of not [caring] or the aesthetic of telling it like it is has become so popular that there's a lot of people who pander to that concept rather than are that concept. Sabrina actually is."

The two, of course, have Taylor Swift in common, but they actually met at a comedy club in New York City in 2022, around the same time Sabrina stood front and center at a Bleachers show at Radio City Music Hall, maybe or maybe not to get his attention.

"I was peeing my pants because I wanted to work with him for my whole life. After that, we, luckily enough, became friends; personalities meshed, and it was only a matter of time," Sabrina told *Rolling Stone*. Jack steered four songs on *Short n' Sweet,* including "Lie to Girls," "Sharpest Tool," "Slim Pickins," and uber-hit "Please Please Please"; for the latter, Jack told Grammy.com, "We were thinking a lot about joy and the kind of fantastical nature of ABBA, Dolly [Parton], and ELO." What kismet

Jack Antonoff and Sabrina together onstage at a Grammy Museum event in Los Angeles, California, August 2, 2024.

then when Dolly ended up appearing on a remix of the track on the album's deluxe edition in 2025.

Sabrina has gushed about Jack "he's one of the most talented people I've ever met. When he's in a room, he's able to literally touch every instrument and make it sound magical." She also told Apple Music that working with Jack is downright "fun . . . he's really playful with chords . . . that just brings my love of music back." So of course, when the producer and his wife, actress Margaret Qualley, showed up at Sabrina's Short n' Sweet Tour stop in LA in November 2024, she had to "arrest" them, well Margaret at least. "I'm almost so confident you can *produce* someone even hotter than you," Sabrina joked.

PART 4
THE SABRINA SHOW

There's no question Sabrina Carpenter knows how to leave *quite an impression*—as we've seen over the past three years, particularly in concert. After being a part of Taylor's blitzkrieg from August 2023 to March 2024, the buzz built quickly as audiences witnessed the now-grownup Disney star turn into a fiery pop star ready to take her latest *Short n' Sweet* album on her own tour.

The attention on Sabrina really came to a head in early 2024, starting with that unforgettable set at Coachella in April. The festival, around since 1999, has long been a dream booking for any artist. It's a total tastemaker affair that can launch careers or rebrand artists overnight: Doja Cat, Raye, and Billie Eilish are a few recent examples.

It helps that Coachella is one of the first mass events of the calendar year, months before Lollapalooza, Bonnaroo, and Governors Ball, literally setting the stage for everything that comes after. It also helps that where it's held–in Indio, California–is a short road trip from Los Angeles. Coachella "takes artists from cool to A-list," *Billboard* has said, adding that it "looms over all others as the biggest, flashiest, most ground-breaking, and most influential live music event in North America."

For Sabrina Carpenter, Coachella was one of the most influential events of her career to date. It was so beautifully timed that it felt like divine intervention had to have played a part. The first-weekend set came the literal day after she dropped "Espresso" as a single on April 11. Sabrina debuted the track live at Coachella and had tongues lapping it up.

PREVIOUS
Sabrina Carpenter during a moment of her Short n' Sweet Tour at Barclays Center in New York City, September 30, 2024.

The Desert Sun keenly picked up on the elevated look of Sabrina's Coachella set, saying, "The production value was just as important and impressive as the vocals." It was one of the first times a big budget was on the table, and the first where a narrative drove the backdrop. The chosen vibe, a heartbreak motel motif, came courtesy of the same design company, STUFISH, that developed the Short n' Sweet Tour's adult dollhouse. Sabrina's Coachella production served as a great foreshadow for what was to come just six months later on her headline tour.

"Church bells rang to signal the start of the show. The giant screen TVs played the intro to a fake 1950s noir film called *The Wreckage* starring Carpenter," *The Desert Sun* recalled, setting the scene of the Coachella set. "Her character drove frantically in the middle of the night before crashing into a motel. That motel then served as the backdrop of her set, along with the wrecked vehicle sticking out of the side."

When all was said and done, Sabrina's domination at Coachella set off a domino-toppling series of events. First was "Espresso" debuting on the *Billboard* Hot 100, eventually peaking at No. 3. Her previous *Emails I Can't Send* hit, "Feather," also reached its highest point on the chart, No. 24, that very same day, but the timing was no *coincidence*. *Hypebot*, an outlet that reports on music trends and technologies, has the receipts to back up what's deemed "The Coachella Effect." As "one of the most culturally influential music events across the globe" and "a major cultural zeitgeist . . . that [gives] many artists the opportunity to grow their audiences," the proof is in the data.

Hypebot has claimed that artists' Chartmetric data—a comprehensive analytical platform to simultaneously gauge streaming, social, and audience engagement—increased by an average of 13 percent for 2024 Coachella performers. For Sabrina, she was the artist with the second-biggest gain, coming in at 40.9 percent. Along with fellow Coachella breakout act Chappell Roan's similar gains, *Hypebot* said, "Some of the most talked-about acts this year were young burgeoning female pop stars . . . the success of these artists is a clear sign that [the] music industry is undergoing a pop girl revolution."

Sabrina appears at Coachella Valley Music and Arts Festival at Empire Polo Club in Indio, California, April 12, 2024.

Sabrina 2.0 Emerges

Having piqued the public's interest at Coachella and the pivotal moments that came before it, Sabrina was in an incredibly fortuitous position to reinvent herself while eyes were still on her, and she and her team pounced on the opportunity with *Short n' Sweet*. In an examination posted on the *Venice Music* website, titled, "Sabrina Carpenter Marketing Case Study: Rebranding As A Superstar," the firm claimed that *Short n' Sweet* was not just a blitzkrieg of an album but also had a whole intelligent rollout behind it that other artists can pull from. Sabrina's 2.0 launch, they said, "serves as a masterclass in how to strategically evolve an artist's public image."

Venice Music's analysis said the approach was three-pronged: Bring in some good-old-fashioned Hollywood references, add in cheeky humor, and give off some undeniable romance. Coupled with aspirational music videos like the "Nonsense" visual, it was the perfect recipe for idol worship—the whole "guys want her, girls want to be her" adage.

"By leaning into her Hollywood roots, Sabrina Carpenter embraced her cinematic flair, using film references and actor appearances to align her image with classic Hollywood glamor," the marketing study opined. "Simultaneously, she maintained a playful, self-aware humor that kept her approachable and relatable, particularly to a younger, Gen Z audience. Lastly, Carpenter's exploration of romance—through themes of love, heartbreak, and sensuality—gave her image a mature, sophisticated edge that resonated deeply with her audience."

The buzz really started with "Espresso." The chorus is so unbelievably catchy, it's basically been glued into our frontal lobes for the better part of a year. With it, Sabrina cornered the market on subliminal marketing and also gave TikTok plenty of fodder to help spread it around (a trait that's now becoming her specialty).

A Whole Lot of Word Play

Vulture interviewed a linguistics expert to understand why we can't stop sipping on (or chanting) "Espresso"—and the science behind it is rather interesting. "The reduplication of the word *that* [in the chorus] is there to foster a sense of playfulness, to catch attention," Ekkarat Ruanglertsilp told the magazine. He's a linguistics professor at Hampton University who has researched how language interplays with pop music. In general, he says, there's a ton to read between the lines in the lyrics, even if some want to dismiss it as a flash-in-the-pan pop song.

"Another way to look at it: Could she be seen as a femme fatale here? I mean, it's not a new concept. A lot of pop artists have done this before: Britney, Madonna, Beyoncé, Ariana Grande. So when we just listen to the lyrics without being critical, it might mean portraying this woman as being promiscuous or something like that. But if we *really* look at the lyrics—if we look at the social ideologies behind these words, behind these linguistic strategies—we can see that Sabrina is the one holding the power."

Intelligent as it may be, the intent was just really getting people hooked on "Espresso"—and it worked. "I think that's the whole point . . . It's like somewhat addictive," she declared to *The Hollywood Reporter*." And after it got stuck in her own head, she told *Rolling Stone*, "I decided to put that burden on other people."

In theory, Sabrina said *Short n' Sweet* is "the hot older sister" of *Emails I Can't Send*, referring to it as her "second 'big girl' album." It also followed the path of *Emails* and even earlier songs like the cheeky "Sue Me," where the motive was "taking personal situations in my life and being able to turn them into art," she told *Vogue*. "[That was] always a way of healing myself, and also understanding those situations a bit better."

There was a difference in her state of mind between making *Emails I Can't Send* and *Short n' Sweet*: this time around, Sabrina tackled the situations with humor. "I cried every day then. I don't cry every day now," she shared with *Rolling Stone*.

"I think that's the whole point . . . It's like somewhat addictive."

> *"Why is humor the thing that sticks with us? Those are the memories we really do hold on to for such a long time, longer than the moments we were fighting each other."*

"When you're at the point in your life where you're always at your wits' end, everything is funny; everything can be funny because it's all stupid," she shared with Apple Music. "Why is humor the thing that sticks with us? Those are the memories we really do hold on to for such a long time, longer than the moments we were fighting each other. Whenever I have fights with people, we forget what we were fighting about, but if we have an inside joke it lasts forever."

It seems like Sabrina was working to share many memorable jokes, as there are plenty of them across *Short n' Sweet*. "Bed Chem" actually came out of a shared Airbnb experience that turned into a "had to be there" moment with Sabrina's best friend Paloma. "We're like talking and we fell asleep together at the exact same time . . . no one was kicking, no one was snoring or kicking . . . and I was like, 'We have really good bed chem,'" she recounted in NPR's *Tiny Desk* session.

And with "Don't Smile," that was actually one of the first songs Sabrina didn't write from a firsthand experience, but rather it came from helping a friend going through a rough breakup and joking together about how much they hated the common colloquialism, "don't cry because it's over, smile because it happened." As Sabrina told Apple Music's Zane Lowe, "That saying is something that's on like every Pinterest board, on every sewn pillow . . . and I was like [forget] that."

So, what doesn't she find funny? "People," she told Zane Lowe. "There [are] so many people I don't find funny . . . That's what honestly inspired so many lyrics on the album, people not being funny."

"Taking personal situations in my life and being able to turn them into art, [that was] always a way of healing myself."

She Loves a Bit of Flirtation

In addition to humor, Sabrina's flirty side really came out on *Short n' Sweet* as she continued to play around with explicit expression—this time though, not just in tour outros, but on record . . . for all time. "Over the last year, I've heard from a lot of people, like, 'Wow, she's just the [flirtiest] girl alive,' because sometimes in my songs, I say some crazy things . . . But I'm actually a very normal amount of [flirty]," she joked with *Vanity Fair*. "It's just a matter of not taking things too seriously. I love play on words and I love funny innuendos; it's just always been something that makes me laugh."

> "It's just a matter of not taking things too seriously. I love play on words and I love funny innuendos; it's just always been something that makes me laugh."

PREVIOUS
Sabrina attends a *Time* 100 event at Pier 59 in New York City, October 9, 2024.

Some people did take it too seriously though. A headline in the *New York Post* in August 2024 read, "Parents freak over Sabrina Carpenter's [flirty] new album: 'Inappropriate for children.'"

But was it not age-appropriate for twenty-five-year-old Sabrina? "When I was younger, I think I'd almost feel pressure to write about mature subject matter because of the people around you being like, 'This is something that is cool and what works.' I didn't do it until I felt like it was actually authentic to me," she told *Rolling Stone*. "Those real moments where I'm just a twenty-five-year-old girl who's super [flirty] are as real as when I'm going through a heartbreak and I'm miserable and I don't feel like a person."

Regardless of anyone else's thoughts, Sabrina was not about to start censoring herself. "I don't want to live out of fear that I might upset anyone," she told Apple Music.

One person who was not taken aback by Sabrina's evolving adult themes in her lyrics was her long-time vocal coach Eric Vetro, who told *People* that hearing the tracks on *Short n' Sweet* was actually on brand for the Sabrina he's known for years. "She always had a fun sense of humor that was a tiny bit risqué in general. It didn't surprise me . . . She rides that line really, really well. She never falls into anything that's trashy . . . It's sexy and fun, all the innuendos."

As Sabrina discovered, sex and sarcasm sell. But, beyond the ostentatiousness, there're also really vulnerable moments on *Short n' Sweet*. The song that makes Sabrina the most emotional? "Sharpest Tool." "I've always yearned . . . to care enough about a person or a situation or a relationship in my life that it provokes that much feeling in me. Maybe it's because it goes back to being an actress," she told Zach Sang of Apple Music. "There's this part of me that just probably over-fantasizes and romanticizes everything."

With so many layers and deeply personal themes, *Short n' Sweet* became a magnifying mirror for Sabrina. "I'll never forget this album for teaching me so much about myself," she told Zane Lowe, adding that she also holds herself accountable. "I'll call myself out just as much as I'll call out someone else," she said.

That raw honesty resonated with others too, catapulting *Short n' Sweet* to the upper echelons of pop music in 2024. The album was hailed as setting "a high bar for big pop" by *Pitchfork,* which celebrated the record for being "cheeky, clever, and expertly executed." *Variety* called it "masterful." *New York Times* said the album is "gloriously sly and merciless." *Paper* called Sabrina "the best new pop star," and *Rolling Stone* cautioned, "do not underestimate Ms. Carpenter's pen."

"I'll never forget this album for teaching me so much about myself."

The album's cinematic videos for "Espresso," "Taste," and "Please Please Please" also cast their own kind of spell and pushed *Short n' Sweet* further into the pop culture web. In total, the album spent four weeks at the No. 1 spot on the *Billboard* 200 album chart. All twelve tracks were incredibly placed in various spots on the *Billboard* Hot 100, including three in the top five. It's a rare feat to have a full album's worth of songs charting on *Billboard* at the same time, an accomplishment that only the likes of Olivia Rodrigo and Taylor Swift have seen in the recent past. Eight of *Short n' Sweet*'s tracks have also either been certified gold or platinum by the RIAA® and the album itself has been certified 2x Platinum.

"I've never really been on charts until quite recently, so it's a newfound, like . . . I'm *interested*," she told *The Guardian* of her unreal success with the album. "It's not the reason I write music and it's not the reason I'll ever write music. It's like the sprinkles on top of the sundae."

FOLLOWING
Sabrina performing with Bleachers during the 10th Annual Ally Coalition Talent Show in New York City, December 17, 2024.

"I've always yearned . . . to care enough about a person or a situation or a relationship in my life that it provokes that much feeling in me."

Her World's a Stage

Just a month after *Short n' Sweet* took over the world on August 23, 2024, the pop star took the show on the road and delivered another intimate affair that spoke to the day-one diehards. For ninety minutes every night, Sabrina invited fans home to her pearly two-story penthouse and turned them into a captivated audience as they watched the entertaining slumber party play out over twenty-one songs.

TV show cameras were capturing it all, too, for the audience at home. Well, not really. It was just part of the nostalgic '70s variety show motif of the tour, which was accentuated by overhead signs in the stadiums that alerted the sold-out crowds that the whole thing was being "filmed in front of a live studio audience." (And anyway, the thousands of fans streaming it live for TikTok had basically the same result.)

Looking at the overwhelmingly positive reviews from the tour, many likened the charades to *The Truman Show* meets Polly Pocket fantasy meets Barbie Dreamhouse spectacular. And fans got the assignment, showing up in feather boas, platform boots, various shades of pink, and tons of sparkle as if it was required attire. Was it over the top? Sure. But in the best way possible.

In the post–COVID-19 pandemic world of live entertainment, a bare-bones setup is the biggest faux pas of all. As Taylor, Beyoncé, Olivia, and the master of shtick, Chappell Roan, all know, a strong concept has become the crown on which pop queens build reputations—and careers. Sabrina just naturally followed course across her own fifty-one-date global trek, and in the process, saw her career grow in real-time.

Four days after the Short n' Sweet Tour kicked off, on September 27, the album was certified platinum. By this time, it had only been just over a month since the album dropped. It's not a surprising phenomenon—the more an artist tours, and shocks and awes across the spectrum of traditional media and social media coverage, the more they rise to the top. As *Billboard* reported, 2023 brought a huge swell for concerts with the top 100 tours grossing 50 percent more than they did in 2019, which also resulted in an explosion of streaming returns. In most cases, pop artists were the victors, seeing a massive 200-percent-plus increase in streaming numbers. In Sabrina's case, the fact that "Espresso" was *the* soundtrack of the summer and, a few months prior, won over Coachella, also helped.

Carrying on that momentum, Sabrina tapped the same creative team that developed her heartbreak motel concept from Coachella to come up with an equally compelling design for the Short n' Sweet Tour, namely top-tier stage designers STUFISH plus her sister Sarah who acted as creative director. STUFISH is a UK team of "entertainment architects" that have been behind some of the most iconic tour designs in pop music history. Their list of clients dates as far back as Janet Jackson's iconic Rhythm Nation Tour in 1990 to Lady Gaga's Born This Way Ball in 2012, Beyoncé's 2023 Renaissance Tour, and several of Madonna's conceptual packages as seen on MDNA (2012), Madame X (2019), and The Celebration Tour (2023).

STUFISH has said the design for Sabrina's Short n' Sweet Tour was meant to "evoke a playful, fantasy environment" that "plays out as a whole evening from a sunset slumber party, through the cocktail hour... and into the disco party, culminating in the morning after."

House Beautiful noted how Sabrina carried over her trademark Hollywood glam/retro aesthetic into the design of her four-room stage home, which offered a flurry of on-point mid-century details. There's the '60s-era "Malm-like fireplace" in the living room, a vintage circular bed, a spiral staircase, and the total throwback conversation pit shaped like a heart with accompanying pillows at the edge of the stage. But it's the bathroom that was the focus of the tour. And the one Sabrina had the most fun playing with. *House Beautiful* said, "It looks like something out of a Marilyn Monroe movie," noting the feminine-shaped curves of the soaking tub, the heart-shaped mirror (that matched the toilet lid), and a shell-shaped sink. The resounding consensus from many fans was, "Can we live here?"

> "[The tour] evokes a playful, fantasy environment [that] plays out as a whole evening from a sunset slumber party, through the cocktail hour... and into the disco party, culminating in the morning after."

Sabrina during a stop of the Short n' Sweet Tour at Madison Square Garden in New York City, September 29, 2024.

Not Everyone Was a Fan

In the crowd for the kickoff night, Sabrina's dad and grandfather were proudly taking it all in. Which, knowing the sequence of events, may sound cringe to some. "My fans online are like, I can't believe she's bending over in front of her grandparents!" Sabrina told *Time*. "I'm like, girl, they are not paying attention to that. They're just like, I can't believe all these people are here."

Some fans also had reservations about taking their own family members to Sabrina's latest tour, particularly those who bought tickets with parents during the tour's early presale in June, two months before *Short n' Sweet* and all its foul-mouthed glory was fully out in the open. "Please wish me luck, I'm going to this tour with my mom who wants to bring my grandmother if my sister can't make it," posted one TikToker. "Be careful about taking your parents to a Sabrina Carpenter concert," another YouTuber cautioned, suggesting to "distract" mom and dad before the outro of "Bed Chem" or right before the line in "Juno" where Sabrina imitates her favorite positions. "Concert tickets need to be sold AFTER the album comes out," a jilted parent wrote on social media.

> *"The scariest thing in the world is getting up on a stage in front of that many people and having to perform as if it's nothing. If the one thing that helps you do that is the way you feel comfortable dressing, then that's what you've got to do."*

Sabrina wasn't having any of it; however, there was *one* apology she made to a mom who posted a duet of "Please Please Please" with her young child on TikTok and demonstrated how the tot loved to come in strong on the curse word. "Just dropped the clean I am so sorry," Sabrina responded. But beyond dropping a PG version of the track, sanitizing the lyric to the limp alt take, "little sucker," Sabrina cautioned all the other haters to simply stay at home. To be fair, the "TV cameras" on the tour did provide a notice that "parental discretion is advised" right before Sabrina launched into the hush-hush "Bed Chem."

Even so, Sabrina told *Time*, "You'll still get the occasional mother that has a strong opinion on how you should be dressing. And to that I just say, don't come to the show and that's OK. It's unfortunate that it's ever been something to criticize, because truthfully, the scariest thing in the world is getting up on a stage in front of that many people and having to perform as if it's nothing. If the one thing that helps you do that is the way you feel comfortable dressing, then that's what you've got to do."

The Short n' Sweet Tour choreography was equally and brilliantly provocative, thanks to the handiwork of Jasmine Badie, who has worked with Sabrina since 2021. Jasmine also clapped back at the criticism the pop star received for her suggestive routines, saying Sabrina approaches her sexuality in dance in the same tongue-in-cheek manner she applies to her lyrics.

"You have to know how to read to understand what she's saying. You have to know what innuendos are. You have to know what synonyms are. You have to know what symbolism is," Jasmine, who has also worked with Megan Thee Stallion and Cardi B, explained in an interview with *Rolling Stone*. She pointed out other covert provocateurs like Marvin Gaye to further her case. "He would sing about making love to someone and having sex, but he wasn't saying it," Jasmine added. "[Sabrina's] singing the same kinds of things . . . She's saying it in a classy way . . . It takes a smart person to be able to do that." So, haters, save your dumb blonde jokes for someone else.

Sabrina Carpenter performs at MTV's Video Music Awards at the UBS Arena in Elmont, New York, September 11, 2024.

FOLLOWING
Sabrina attends the 2025 Met Gala, with the theme, "Superfine: Tailoring Black Style," in New York City, May 5, 2025.

"You'll still get the occasional mother that has a strong opinion on how you should be dressing. And to that I just say, don't come to the show."

Under the Covers

Ten years ago, Sabrina started her journey by posting covers to her YouTube page, and she wasn't about to stop the practice on her Short n' Sweet Tour. Here's who she covered live on stage during the US and Europe legs (naturally, determined by a game of Spin the Bottle):

"Mamma Mia" by ABBA

"That Don't Impress Me Much" by Shania Twain

"Kiss Me" by Sixpence None the Richer

"Material Girl" by Madonna

"9 to 5" by Dolly Parton

"Hopelessly Devoted to You" by Olivia Newton-John

"Super Freak" by Rick James

"Come on Eileen" by Dexys Midnight Runners

"Lady Marmalade" by LaBelle

Sabrina performs at the Governors Ball Music Festival at Flushing Meadows Corona Park in New York City, June 8, 2024.

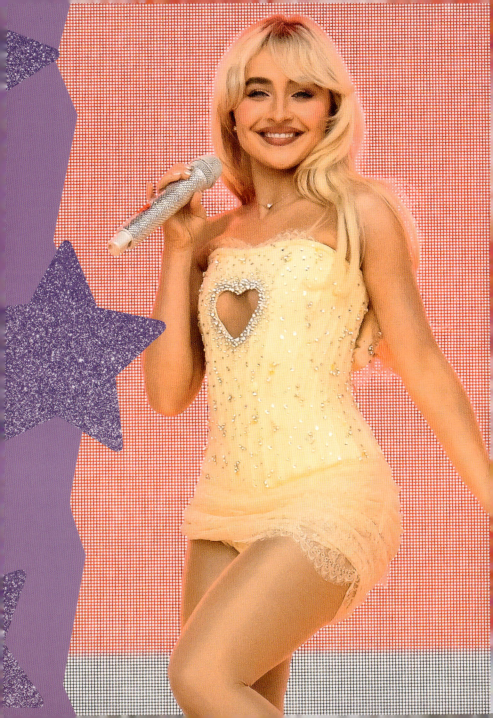

Yes, This Is Live

The controversy spawned by the Short n' Sweet Tour was not even the first time on the tour there was some uproar. A week after the jaunt kicked off, there were some rumors popping up on TikTok that Sabrina wasn't fully singing live. "Hate to say it but 30 percent lip singing [sic] 30 percent backing track 40 percent singing," one person posted. Ever-active TikToker Sabrina herself took note of the comment and quickly entered the chat. "I sing live every show 100 percent," she commented. "Would you like to speak to my audio engineers?" And then, to prove her point, she took it a step further by removing backing tracks on some of the songs and turning up her mic on others for subsequent dates of the tour, as reported by *Teen Vogue*. Talk about a mic drop.

"I sing live every show 100 percent. Would you like to speak to my audio engineers?"

Others took issue with the fact that Sabrina chose to ignore her first-born albums when it came time to create the Short n' Sweet Tour setlist. "For the people who love those early records and listen to them, I love you for that," Sabrina told *Variety*. "But I personally feel a sense of separation from them, largely due to the shift in who I am as a person and as an artist, pre-pandemic and post-pandemic." She added in a chat with Apple Music, "I've gotten to this place now where there's so many *other* songs that I want to sing."

Rather, each night followed the same twenty-one-song rollout, except for the revolving "surprise cover song," and in general featured all twelve songs from her *Short n' Sweet* album, plus eight from *Emails I Can't Send* and the deluxe edition, *Fwd:*. Cover songs were determined by an apropos game of Spin the Bottle, including some '70s and '80s hits like Dolly Parton's "9 to 5," Madonna's "Material Girl," and ABBA's "Mamma Mia."

USA Today called the show a "live-action *Cinderella*," rationalizing that "the reigning princess of pop, after a decade of ascending to the crown, is like Disney royalty come to life." But really, the show would be better classified as the departure from Disney in her repertoire—and the birth of Sabrina "make me Juno" Carpenter.

While Sabrina retired the "Nonsense" outros on the Short n' Sweet Tour, she did add in other customizable details, making each show feel like their own unique take of the touring sitcom. In addition to the cover song roulette, Sabrina switched up the colors of her bathrobe-bearing corsets. She had different lyrics printed on her tights each night. She handcuffed different hotties. And she crafted unique intros for "Espresso." In Boston, it was, "Should we talk about how it would've been different if they called it the Boston Espresso Party?" In Seattle, it was an obvious plug: "Seattle must have a drink. They must have a drink. They are so famous for it. I don't know what it is, but maybe it's . . . espresso?"

Also in Seattle, just a day after the latest US presidential election, Sabrina addressed a more serious issue. "I just wanna say, life is so unfortunately crazy right now, and so for everybody in here to come here to escape, I hope we can be a moment of peace for you and a moment of safety," she said to the crowd, per the *Seattle Times*. "I'm sorry about our country. And to the women, I love you so, so, so, so, so much." The paper also reported that earlier in the tour, Sabrina helped to register 35,814 voters thanks to their work with the nonprofit HeadCount, with the pop star "engaging more voters than any other artist in 2024," according to *Variety*.

For the Halloween show in Dallas, Sabrina came back from each quick change to unveil a new character costume, including a Playboy Bunny, Tinkerbell, and Sandy from *Grease*. And, as *Entertainment Weekly* reported, "More Halloween-themed tricks and treats included the crew wearing blond Carpenter-esque wigs backstage, the railing of the grand staircase being covered in a creepy spiderweb, and the singer performing 'Slim Pickins' surrounded by pumpkins, black cats, and other paranormal paraphernalia."

When it came time for the three-date Los Angeles finale, a slew of celebrities also packed the arena including Katy Perry, John Mayer, Noah Cyrus, Robin Thicke, Blue Ivy Carter (who had painted lip-smacking icons all over herself), *Girl Meets World* costar Danielle Fishel, and a series of famous folks who were "arrested" during "Juno." On night one was *Bottoms* star Rachel Sennott; night two was Marcello Hernandez aka *Saturday Night Live*'s Domingo; and night three was Jack Antonoff's talented wife, *Substance* actress Margaret Qualley. Atlanta also had a special person of honor as Sabrina "arrested" *Stranger Things* actress

Millie Bobby Brown. And in Europe, there was *Desperado* actress Salma Hayek and singer Emma "Baby Spice" Bunton.

The guest appearances just kept coming, especially at the first LA show when none other than Christina Aguilera crashed the set for an incredible duet of "What A Girl Wants" and "Ain't No Other Man." The two pop stars had, two months prior, collaborated on a twenty-fifth-anniversary celebration of Christina's debut album where they sang and recorded "What A Girl Wants."

By the end of her tour, Sabrina was gathering all sorts of fast new friends and fans, which was kismet. As she shared with a crowd in New York, "I got to write *Short n' Sweet* by just having a big ol' [freaking] laugh with my friends. And now everyone's in the room having a laugh with their friends. Hopefully, we can keep that going."

FOLLOWING
Sabrina accepts the BRIT Award for Global Success at The O2 Arena in London, England, March 1, 2025.

"I got to write **Short n' Sweet** by just having a big ol' [freaking] laugh with my friends. And now everyone's in the room having a laugh with their friends. Hopefully, we can keep that going."

An Extra Shot

Taking One for the Team

In her appearance on *Hot Ones*, Sabrina admitted she's not really a big "sports kind of girl." And really, she just roots for "whoever wants me to sing the National Anthem," she told *Open House Party*. But did her admissions lead to one of the biggest curses of 2024? Some people think so. "The Sabrina Carpenter Curse is sweeping through all major sports," the blog *Barstool Sports* lamented on Instagram. "The Sabrina Carpenter Curse Is Wrecking Sports Teams Worldwide," read a headline in *Vice*. The article explained that every time the pop star wore an official jersey during a local tour stop, that team ended up losing.

And it wasn't just once or twice. There's been at least four documented instances. It started somewhere around July when Sabrina wore an England soccer jersey as the team was getting ready to play a EuroCup game against Spain and lost. When Sabrina wore a gemmed-out Maple Leafs jersey in Toronto that September, the team lost their home opener against Montreal.

It didn't have to be official gear either; any sports apparel was cursed apparently. When Sabrina wore a Dallas Cowboys sweatshirt, they fared an embarrassing loss of forty-seven to nine against the Detroit Lions. Even her *own* home team wasn't immune: Sabrina donned a No. 69 Phillies jersey as the baseball club entered the playoffs and—you guessed it—lost against New York. Many fans took to social media to try to save their favorite clubs, with a chorus of "Please Please Please" stop wearing our teams' jerseys.

Sabrina sings the National Anthem at Dodger Stadium in California, July 26, 2016.

Who knew, out of all the collaborations that brought us some of the best Sabrina songs and shows around the world, it would be sports that just didn't mix? Maybe there is one thing our five-foot (1.5 m) girl can't do.

PART 5

A BUSY WOMAN

You may now have a better understanding of Sabrina Carpenter at this point—whether it's her rather typical upbringing, no-[cares]-given artistry, or ongoing vertical challenges. But there are some other random things that are important to know about the pop star. There's the fact that she's a huge Harry Potterhead, that she listens to the Bee Gees every single day. She also loves making handmade cards with stickers and glitter. Her life goal is to sit with Rihanna on a couch, watching *That '70s Show*. She's allergic to just about everything, including grass, horses, almonds, and cheap jewelry ("my ears bleed," she told *WIRED*). She loves dessert and ends most days with milkshakes. And friendships are one of the most important things to her—if you don't have a solid circle, she'll actually judge you for it.

"When I start dating someone, or meet someone for the first time, I like to know how long their friendships are. I think it says so much about a person," she shared with Apple Music. In fact, she put Sean Evans on the spot with her friendship litmus test on *Hot Ones* before she felt comfortable moving on in the hot wing challenge. "Do you have a lot of friends?" she quizzed him. "I ask the question because if you feel like you have good friends then I trust you and we're good . . . If you have long relationships, then I'm fine."

> "When I start dating someone, or meet someone for the first time, I like to know how long their friendships are. I think it says so much about a person."

PREVIOUS
Sabrina Carpenter attends the MTV Video Music Awards at the Prudential Center in Newark, New Jersey, September 12, 2023.

Sabrina has not been shy when gushing about her friendships. We know all about the mutual admiration between her and Taylor. And every so often, we're learning more about her best friend, Paloma Sandoval, who was the initial inspiration behind "Bed Chem" and appeared in the "Nonsense" music video. Their friendship has been on full display on social media, too, whether they're dancing together at Coachella, playing with puppies in a parking lot, or reading motivational signs at Buc-ee's.

We can't forget *Kissing Booth* star Joey King who Sabrina has known for a good decade—she cast her, too, in the "Sue Me" video. Apparently, Joey and Sabrina make each other cry (in a good way). "I got to see my wife perform in Chi Town last night and I cried of course, she's just the shortest and sweetest pop star I've ever seen. I might let her make me Juno," Joey shared after seeing Sabrina on a Short n' Sweet Tour stop. "My wife got married and I wept and wept. I felt so immensely lucky to be part of your special day," Sabrina posted in an Instagram carousel of snaps taken from Joey's wedding day.

As you may have gathered, if Sabrina likes someone, she often hard launches their relationship by featuring them in her music videos: Rowan Blanchard in "Seamless," her sister Sarah in "Eyes Wide Open," Paloma and her other bestie Whitney Peak in "Nonsense," Joey in "Sue Me," and most recently, Jenna Ortega in "Taste," and Barry Keoghan in "Please Please Please" are all prime examples.

"I knew immediately I wanted my best friends to be in the video, and I wanted us to play our own boyfriends because the song is just too fun for the video not to be a riot," Sabrina told *Rolling Stone* of the "Nonsense" casting (or double casting, as it was). There's a levity Sabrina finds in featuring her favorite people in the productions, which also draws out her most ridiculous personas. "In the Sabrina Cinematic Universe, women never die. Men, unfortunately, suffer most of the losses. This video, in particular, it's almost comical how the women still don't die," she said of "Taste," where she and Jenna (another old Disney pal) use chain saws and machetes to obliterate each other.

So who could be next? Maybe Chappell Roan, Christina Aguilera, Taylor, or re-teaming with Meghan Trainor? Now that Sabrina's friend requests continue growing as she gets sign-offs from megastars, the possibilities are wide-open and likely, just an actual email away.

She's Got the Look

The other way in which music videos have elevated Sabrina into a new tier is her high-fashion-style. For the "Feather" video, Sabrina based the whole concept around the marquee black Carolina Herrera dress she wore in several scenes. "Basically, the idea for the video came from the funeral look," she told *Cosmopolitan*.

When *Vogue* paid a visit to the set of "Please Please Please" in 2024, the star opened up her fashion look book, which included a hooded dress from Alaïa, a structured corset dress from Dilara Findikoglu, and a furry pink coat from Alexandre Vauthier couture. "I always like to heighten fashion and [the] storyline in my videos, it's playtime for me," she told the magazine.

"I always like to heighten fashion and [the] storyline in my videos, it's playtime for me."

The Big Bangs Theory

There's never been a time in history that women have wanted to cut their bangs as much as they have over the last three years. Not until "Sabrina Carpenter bangs" took over Google and TikTok. The star has perfected the look of the swept Brigitte Bardot curtain bangs, "lush, thick, and perfectly curled under no matter how she's wearing her hair," said *Teen Vogue*.

It all came about for Sabrina the same way bangs do for most of us: a breakup. "I literally cut my bangs 'cause someone broke my heart and I was just like, 'I have to do something,'" she told *Vanity Fair*. "I'm not usually one of those people that has to make rash decisions when their feelings are hurt but that was my first real heartbreak and so I guess it just sparked that initial like, 'I have to do something different.'"

Fortunately for her, it was a wise decision as the look totally suits her. "They give a refined and chic vibe," Noelle Salon said on their blog. The salon also said that the bangs accent Sabrina's favorite facial feature, her cheekbones, which are often accented by a prominent touch of blush.

While there are plenty of how-to videos out there on how to DIY the Sabrina bang, it might be best to take a tip from her own hairstylist, Scott King. As he told *Fashionista*, "Make sure the shortest piece is right in the middle, just above the bridge of your nose—about where the bottom of your eyebrow is—and that it gradually gets longer on each side to about the top of the cheekbones."

Sabrina at the *Variety* Power of Young Hollywood Event in California, August 10, 2023.

Sabrina's stylist, Ron Hartleben, shared with *Vogue* that there's been a flip of the fashion switch lately. "We've also been working together for two years now, and she's totally more mature than when we did our first video together ["Because I Liked a Boy"]. She's come more into her womanhood and is even more confident now," he said. "She believes in what she has to offer the world, and [in] her artistry, so I wanted to elevate the fashion in the same way."

That confidence has been brewing in Sabrina over the past few years (remember when she boldly appeared in the Savage X Fenty Show in 2021?) and has directly correlated to an openness not only in her lyrics but also in her more daring looks. But she'd be the first to admit it took a while to get there. Sabrina's been doing red carpets for ten years and her style has naturally evolved in that time, in the same way she's been promoted from the pages of *Teen Vogue* to regular *Vogue*. "I don't want to remember my first red carpet. I think I wore arm bands," she joked with the teen edition of the magazine. But "If I didn't wear the hideous things I wore when I was thirteen, whatever fedora I had, I don't think I would've been the same person I am today," she conceded to *Interview*.

"She believes in what she has to offer the world, and [in] her artistry, so I wanted to elevate the fashion in the same way."

In her latest era, Sabrina has become more than just a fashion icon, though; she's become an influencer. "She's boosting brand awareness on the red carpet," *Vogue* said in an August 2024 article, profiling Sabrina's fashion impact. "At her second Met Gala appearance in May [2024], Carpenter wore an Oscar de la Renta gown with a black bodice and an orchid-inspired voluminous, satin skirt. Her three posts concerning the dress on Instagram generated $6.65 million in earned media value," the magazine added.

She's been a huge boost for Ukrainian brand Frolov too, opting for their signature heart cut-out dresses for The Eras Tour and several other pieces across 2023. "It really just shines on stage in a way I love," Sabrina told *Vogue* in a separate interview. "They make such beautiful cutouts that feel sturdy and secure, so I don't question moving in them." Her endorsement of the brand and her overall aspirational nature perked up Gen Z, who took an interest in the under-the-radar designer and had them scrambling on the production line. "We found a huge impact on brand [awareness], especially within the US market. Sabrina did a lot for us as a brand to become more famous in the United States," Frolov told *Vogue*. "What's very important to us is that we have a new, younger audience who became our clients and that the new generation is exploring a Ukrainian brand."

FOLLOWING
Sabrina performs onstage during The BRIT Awards at
The O2 Arena in London, England, March 1, 2025.

"If I didn't wear the hideous things I wore when I was thirteen, whatever fedora I had, I don't think I would've been the same person I am today."

Imitation Flatters Her

Vogue has reported that 67 percent of Sabrina's TikTok following is eighteen to twenty-four years of age with that same demo standing at 57 percent on Instagram. That key following has led to a number of lucrative partnerships for Sabrina, both big-scale and with more approachable brands. The list includes respected fashion houses like Prada (Sabrina is the new face of Prada Beauty in 2025), Versace (starring in their eyewear campaign in the summer of 2024), and Marc Jacobs (the face behind the designer's Sack Bag in 2024). On the other end, she was also recently named Redken's first celebrity brand ambassador, and Sabrina hocks her own line with Scent Beauty, including an espresso-themed eau de parfum launch in 2024 that fans were buying up and spraying all over their bodies to smell something like the goddess in the Starbucks logo. There was also that controversial collaboration with SKIMS for the brand's Fits Everybody and Stretch Lace collections, which *Venice Music*'s case study said was incredibly important as it "marked a significant shift towards a sophisticated, body-positive image."

The study also noted that adding in a number of Hollywood references has helped propel Sabrina in her fame game, such as riffing on *Death Becomes Her* and *Kill Bill* in "Taste" and *Natural Born Killers* in the "Please Please Please" video. "This theme also extended to her fashion choices, which often evoked Old Hollywood glamour, such as her Met Gala appearance[s] and her '50s-inspired looks in the 'Espresso' music video," the reporter added. Since the beginning, Sabrina has been locked in on a vintage feel, continuing a mission to bring new life into old Hollywood glamour. She's said that, if time travel were possible, she'd go back to Paris in the '20s.

Older sisters and that classic vocal coach probably had a lot to do with this influence. "I have so much respect for fashion. I feel like I've grown up around it, and it's such a big part of what I do," she told *Glamour* in 2023, though also noting, "I'm a mess if I don't wear things I feel confident in. Performing is so vulnerable that if you don't feel 100 percent good about what you're in, it's really hard to do it fearlessly . . . Right now, it's about finding my personal sense of style, which I've been trying to carve out recently." She added, "I think I'm in that head space right now where I'm like, 'I'm young, I have to wear this all before it looks a little crazy.'"

> "Performing is so vulnerable that if you don't feel 100 percent good about what you're in, it's really hard to do it fearlessly . . . Right now, it's about finding my personal sense of style."

Sabrina has been living in that young and beautiful headspace and sharing it on stage in a way that makes you truly marvel at her style and effortlessness. She's long believed "what you wear on stage is a reflection of your artistry" (per *Vogue*), and her latest Short n' Sweet Tour looks align with that philosophy, like the ultra-feminine babydoll looks that come from very distinct reference points: Brigitte Bardot, Marilyn Monroe, *Grease*, and *Bye Bye Birdie*. "It's kinda like . . . girlies getting ready," she shared in *Vogue*. Some of those ensembles, per *Time,* have included a black lace catsuit and delicate robe from French designer Patou and a dazzling two-piece halter top and skirt with Swarovski crystal mesh designed by Ludovic de Saint Sernin. Another staple is her girlie platform boots that TikTok has christened, "Sabrina Carpenter shoes."

"Femininity is something that I've always embraced. And if right now that means corsets and garter belts and fuzzy robes or whatever . . . then that's what that means," she told *Time*, while knowing full well it might be different tomorrow. "I change every five minutes . . . I feel like this generation just does," she told Zach Sang. As she has discovered over a ten-plus-year career, nothing is set in stone, and life is a journey of finding yourself in the moment.

"The other day, this guy was like, 'Life is so long. You just have to follow the things that make you feel something, whether that's good or bad,'" Sabrina shared with *Interview*. "And I was like, 'Wow, I always hear life is short.' But it made me really excited about the fact that I'm going to find my way through."

Sabrina attends *SNL50: The Anniversary Special* at 30 Rockefeller Center in New York City, February 16, 2025.

FOLLOWING
Sabrina attends The BRIT Awards at The Intercontinental Hotel in London, England, March 1, 2025.

"The other day, this guy was like, 'Life is so long...' And I was like, 'Wow, I always hear life is short.' But it made me really excited about the fact that I'm going to find my way through."

An Extra Shot

Taking on the World

Sabrina's stunning outward appearance has always been matched by the beauty within. Since she was a young girl, the pop star has committed to a number of charities that are personally meaningful, and where she can pay her good fortune forward.

When Sabrina was a teenager, she often partnered with the Ryan Seacrest Foundation to visit children's hospitals across the country and uplift young spirits. "I was in Philly and I met this little girl named Alison. And she said to me, 'I want to be just like you when I grow up.' And I said, 'Why would you want to do that?'" Sabrina recalled to *People* in 2016. Alison's answer: "Because you're so happy!"

"I think it was so incredible because all those kids are going through so much in their lives—so much more than any of us realize," Sabrina said, "and they're still so positive. That made me incredibly happy—happier than even she thought I was!"

In her ongoing activism work, Sabrina has partnered with the American Red Cross' 2Steps2Minutes campaign, Doctors Without Borders, and voting organization HeadCount. She's also been outspoken in her support of marginalized communities such as having the hard conversations during the time of *The Hate U Give* movie and standing with the LGBTQ+ community.

Sabrina hugs fans during *Good Morning America*'s Summer Concert series in New York City, July 5, 2019.

In 2018, Sabrina contributed a letter to *Billboard* for LGBTQ+ Pride Month, writing in part, "I've been so fortunate that many of my LGBTQ+ fans have felt comfortable enough to confide in me and tell me their stories. When you come to my shows with pride flags, screaming the lyrics at the top of your lungs, I hope you feel an overwhelming rush of love and safety. You set an example for all of us. You have shown that the word 'love' is not defined by anything the society or the government determines. Let us not celebrate you all for only this Pride Month, but spread this love, kindness, and open-hearted spirit that you wear on your sleeves every day."

Most recently, she's created the Sabrina Carpenter Fund via the PLUS1 organization, dedicated to supporting the "well-being of people and animals" and focusing on "mental health, animal welfare, and support for the LGBTQ+ community." As of publication, the fund has raised more than $500,000.

A POETIC CONCLUSION

On February 2, 2025, Sabrina won Best Pop Vocal Album for *Short n' Sweet* at the 67th Annual Grammy Awards. In her speech, she said, "I'm still out of breath from the performance, so I was really not expecting this and all those nominees who were just on the screen are some of my favorite artists in the world and I can't believe I'm nominated against them or even in this room right now . . . This is so special to me and *Short n' Sweet* means the world . . . Thank you, holy [cow]. Bye." Sabrina's Grammy wins (she also won Record of the Year for "Espresso") were just the icing on the cake after an incredible year for the *Short n' Sweet* breakout star.

Before 2024 was even over, Sabrina continued working late, logging a guest spot on *The Late Show With Stephen Colbert,* filming the "ho ho ho-iest" Netflix Christmas special, and orchestrating an acoustic NPR Music *Tiny Desk* session, with a full string section that brought her low cuts and thigh highs to a more-or-less high-brow audience.

If you Googled Sabrina's name over the past year, you'd be met with on-brand kissing emojis and lip-smacking sound effects. Go to any hairstylist and ask what's on trend, and they'd say the "Sabrina bang." You could look like her with those retro-tinged pieces from SKIMS, smell like her with her line from Scent Beauty, and hear her voice literally everywhere you went.

In April, *Yahoo!* published a story that (correctly) predicted Sabrina and Chappell were "pop stars in the making," a feat they'd later celebrate together in Sabrina's Netflix holiday special in which Chappell guest starred to duet on the classic "Last Christmas." By May, Sabrina made

PREVIOUS
Sabrina poses with her Grammys during the 67th annual awards show in Los Angeles, California, February 2, 2025.

her debut on *Saturday Night Live*'s Season 49 finale where she performed a swanky take on "Espresso" and a medley of her previous *Emails* hits, "Feather" and "Nonsense." By the next day, Sabrina was still not over the high, posting a thank-you message to the cast and crew on Instagram and sharing, "I'm sooooo not chill about it and never will be."

By June, Sabrina had her first No. 1 on the *Billboard* Hot 100 chart with "Please Please Please," again taking to socials to revel in the moment: "I'm very immensely grateful so I will surely always remember this day for the rest of my life!" By August, *Short n' Sweet* was unleashed on the world; and by September, it hit the top of the *Billboard* 200 chart and was soon certified platinum by the RIAA®. September was also when she won her first major award for the album, taking home MTV's VMA for Song of the Year for "Espresso."

By October, Sabrina sold out her first headline arena tour and made the cover of the *Time* 100 issue. And by December, in conjunction with her Netflix special, *A Nonsense Christmas*, Sabrina's sleeper holiday EP, *Fruitcake*, (released in 2023) was rebirthed a hit. Sales jumped an uncanny 27,000 percent according to *Forbes*. "There's a strong interest in all things related to the singer and actress," the outlet opined.

♥ *"All those nominees who were just on the screen are some of my favorite artists in the world and I can't believe I'm nominated against them or even in this room right now."*

"Sabrina Carpenter has waited her whole life for this," the *Time* 100 story began. And in so many ways, that truth has become a part of her undying charm—perhaps even more than the eyewink jokes. Sabrina's slow rise to the top is a story for the faithful, the epitome of "good things come to those who wait." Her perseverance to keep at the craft she has been owning since she was ten years old, when she first started writing pop zingers in a makeshift studio in her childhood home, is a testament to hard work paying off. Who more than Sabrina can become the latest *IT* girl, the pièce de résistance in a wild era of pop music? She may only be five feet (1.5 m) tall, but she's already climbed an insurmountable pinnacle of achievements: from Top 40 headliner to fashion icon and pop music's best friend; from a blip in rural Pennsylvania to the shining star of Tinseltown.

On a late 2024 appearance on *The Late Show With Stephen Colbert* (which started with an apropos espresso martini chugging contest), the host asked Sabrina if she was taking the time to enjoy the "rocket ride" she was on, to which she responded, "In five years, probably I'll look back on this moment and be like, 'Wow, so much happened at once,' but it's hard to process it in the moment. I'm just trying to make eye contact with you and be as present as I can," she joked, before taking a more serious, heartfelt tone. "I feel so lucky. Singing is all I've ever wanted to do. Writing songs is my favorite thing in the world, so the fact that I can do it, and people listen is sentimental, but it's a gift so I'm very grateful."

Sabrina attends the *SNL50: The Anniversary Special* at Rockefeller Plaza in New York City, February 16, 2025.

"I feel so lucky. Singing is all I've ever wanted to do. Writing songs is my favorite thing in the world, so the fact that I can do it, and people listen is sentimental, but it's a gift so I'm very grateful."

Discography

Eyes Wide Open

Original Release Date: April 14, 2015

Record Label: Hollywood

Singles:
- "We'll Be The Stars" (January 13, 2015)
- "Eyes Wide Open" (April 7, 2015)

Sales: Not publicly known

EVOLution

Original Release Date: October 14, 2016

Record Label: Hollywood

Singles:
- "On Purpose" (July 29, 2016)
- "Thumbs" (January 3, 2017)

Sales: Not publicly known

Singular: Act I

Original Release Date: November 9, 2018

Record Label: Hollywood

Singles:
- "Almost Love" (June 6, 2018)
- "Sue Me" (November 9, 2018)

Sales: Not publicly known

Singular: Act II

Original Release Date: July 19, 2019

Record Label: Hollywood

Singles:
- "Pushing 20" (March 8, 2019)
- "Exhale" (May 3, 2019)
- "In My Bed" (June 7, 2019)

Sales: Not publicly known

PREVIOUS
Sabrina performs at the 67th Annual Grammy Awards at the Crypto.com Arena in Los Angeles, California, February 2, 2025.

Emails I Can't Send*

Original Release Date: July 15, 2022

Record Label: Island

Singles:

- "Skinny Dipping" (September 9, 2021)
- "Fast Times" (February 18, 2022)
- "Vicious" (July 1, 2022)
- "because i liked a boy" (July 15, 2022)
- "Nonsense" (November 14, 2022)

Sales: One million copies (US)

*A deluxe edition *Emails I Can't Send Fwd:* was released March 17, 2023, and produced the hit "Feather."

Short n' Sweet*

Original Release Date: August 23, 2024

Record Label: Island

Singles:

- "Espresso" (April 11, 2024)
- "Please Please Please" (June 6, 2024)
- "Taste" (August 23, 2024)
- "Bed Chem" (October 8, 2024)

Sales: Two million copies (US)

*A deluxe edition of *Short n' Sweet (Deluxe)* was released on February 14, 2025, and included a country rendition of "Please Please Please" featuring Dolly Parton.

Sabrina has also released two EPs: the *Can't Blame a Girl for Trying* EP in 2014 and *Fruitcake* in 2023.

Filmography

2011
Law & Order: SVU (Role: Paula)

2012
Phineas & Ferb (Voice: Additional Voices)
Noobz (Role: Britney)
Gulliver Quinn (Role: Iris)
The Unprofessional (Role: Harper)

2013
The Goodwin Games (Role: Young Chloe)
Orange is the New Black (Role: Jessica Wedge)
Horns (Role: Young Merrin Williams)
Austin & Ally (Role: Lucy)
Sofia the First (Voice: Princess Vivian)—*the role continued through 2018*

2014
Girl Meets World (Role: Maya Hart)—*the role continued through 2017*

2016
Wander Over Yonder (Voice: Melodie)
Adventures in Babysitting (Role: Jenny Parker)
Walk the Prank (Role: Candace)
Milo's Murphy Law (Voice: Melissa Chase)—*the role continued through 2019*

2018
Mickey and the Roadster Racers (Voice: Nina Glitter)
The Hate U Give (Role: Hailey)
So Close (Role: Jessica)

2019

The Short History of the Long Road (Role: Nola)

Tall Girl (Role: Harper Kreyman)

2020

Royalties (Role: Bailey Rouge)

Work It (Role: Quinn Ackerman)

Clouds (Role: Sammy Brown)

2022

Emergency (Role: Maddy)

Tall Girl 2 (Role: Harper Kreyman)

2024

A Nonsense Christmas with Sabrina Carpenter

BROADWAY

2020

Mean Girls (Role: Cady Heron)

Awards and Nominations

Billboard Music Awards

2024: Top Artist (Nominated)
2024: Top Female Artist (Nominated)
2024: Top Hot 100 Artist (Nominated)
2024: Top Streaming Songs Artist (Nominated)
2024: Top Radio Songs Artist (Nominated)
2024: Top *Billboard* Global 200 Artist (Nominated)
2024: Top *Billboard* Global 200 Song for "Espresso" (Nominated)

BMI Pop Awards

2024: Most Performed Song of the Year for "Nonsense" (Won)
2024: Best New Artist (Nominated)
2024: Record of the Year for "Espresso" (Nominated)

BreakTudo Awards

2018: Artist on the Rise (Nominated)
2019: International Performance for "Pocket Show Universal" (Nominated)
2020: Best Soundtrack for "Let Me Move You" (Nominated)
2021: Anthem of the Year for "Skin" (Nominated)
2022: Anthem of the Year for "Fast Times" (Nominated)

2023: International Video for "Nonsense" (Nominated)
2024: International Female Artist (Nominated)
2024: International Music Video for "Please Please Please" (Nominated)

BRIT Awards

2025: Global Success (Won)
2025: International Artist of the Year (Nominated)

Fragrance Foundation Awards

2023: Fragrance of the Year, Popular for "Sweet Tooth" (Finalist)

Grammy Awards

2025: Best New Artist (Nominated)
2025: Album of the Year for *Short n' Sweet* (Nominated)
2025: Best Pop Vocal Album for *Short n' Sweet* (Won)
2025: Song of the Year for "Please Please Please" (Nominated)
2025: Record of the Year for "Espresso" (Nominated)
2025: Best Pop Solo Performance for "Espresso" (Won)

iHeartRadio Music Awards

2024: Favorite Tour Style (Nominated)
2024: Best Lyrics for "Nonsense" (Nominated)
2025: Song of the Year for "Espresso" (Nominated)
2025: Pop Song of the Year for "Espresso" (Won)
2025: Pop Artist of the Year (Won)
2025: Artist of the Year (Nominated)
2025: Favorite Tour Tradition for "Juno" position (Nominated)
2025: Best Lyrics for "Espresso" (Nominated)
2025: Best Music Video for "Espresso" and "Please Please Please" (Nominated)

MTV Europe Music Awards

2023: Biggest Fans (Nominated)
2024: Best Artist (Nominated)
2024: Best Pop (Nominated)
2024: Biggest Fans (Nominated)
2024: Best US Act (Nominated)
2024: Best Song for "Espresso" (Won)

MTV Video Music Awards

2024: Artist of the Year (Nominated)
2024: Best Pop (Nominated)
2024: Song of the Year for "Espresso" (Won)
2024: Best Editing for "Espresso" (Nominated)
2024: Best Direction for "Please Please Please" (Nominated)
2024: Best Art Direction for "Please Please Please" (Nominated)
2024: Song of Summer for "Please Please Please" (Nominated)

Nickelodeon Kids' Choice Awards

2024: Favorite Ticket of the Year for Emails I Can't Send Tour (Nominated)
2024: Favorite Viral Song for "Espresso" (Nominated)

Radio Disney Music Awards

2015: Best Crush Song for "Can't Blame a Girl for Trying" (Won)
2016: Best Anthem for "Eyes Wide Open" (Won)
2017: Best Crush Song for "On Purpose" (Nominated)
2018: Best Crush Song for "Why" (Nominated)

SCAD Savannah Film Festival

2019: Best Performance for "The Short History of the Long Road" (Won)

Variety Hitmakers

2023: Rising Star Award (Won)

Sources

American Songwriter, "Digital Cover Story: Sabrina Carpenter Makes Necessary Life Edits on 'emails i can't send'," October 2022: https://americansongwriter.com/digital-cover-story-sabrina-carpenter-makes-necessary-life-edits-on-emails-i-cant-send/

AOL Build Series, "Sabrina Carpenter Talks 'Girl Meets World'," December 2017: https://www.youtube.com/watch?v=AnzMDZxXfoE

AOL Build Series, "'I Really Wanted A Locker'—Sabrina Carpenter Talks Missing Out On Regular School," June 2018: https://www.youtube.com/watch?v=OIvssSAPouY

Apple Music, "Sabrina Carpenter: Short n' Sweet, Songwriting & 'Espresso'," August 2024: https://www.youtube.com/watch?v=enaGNnGB99I

Billboard Chart History: https://www.billboard.com/artist/sabrina-carpenter/

Billboard, "Is Sabrina Carpenter Ready to Blow Up? Disney Star Discusses New Single 'Why'," July 2017: https://www.billboard.com/music/pop/sabrina-carpenter-why-interview-single-disney-7857811/

Billboard, "Sabrina Carpenter on Her Mature New Album and Treadmill-Ready Single 'Almost Love'," June 2018: https://www.billboard.com/music/music-news/sabrina-carpenter-almost-love-interview-new-album-singular-8461765/

Billboard, "Sabrina Carpenter: Love Letter to the LGBTQ Community," June 2018: https://www.billboard.com/culture/pride/sabrina-carpenter-gay-pride-love-letter-lgbt-8462312/

Billboard, "Sabrina Carpenter Writes Her Next Chapter: 'I Feel a New Sense of Freedom'," October 2021: https://www.billboard.com/music/pop/sabrina-carpenter-interview-feature-new-album-island-records-9645263/

CBS News Sunday Morning, "Sabrina Carpenter on *Short n' Sweet*," October 2024: https://www.cbs.com/shows/video/T0KwTMrY_087Pbnqojqi7sDPv69cHpMi/

Cosmopolitan, "Sabrina Carpenter's movies and TV shows," July 2024: https://www.cosmopolitan.com/uk/entertainment/a61530991/sabrina-carpenter-movies-tv-shows/

Forbes, "30 Under 30: Sabrina Carpenter," 2021: https://www.forbes.com/profile/sabrina-carpenter/

Glamour, "Sabrina Carpenter on navigating her twenties, finding her voice through music and 'adding to her story' with *Emails I Can't Send* deluxe edition," March 2023: https://www.glamourmagazine.co.uk/article/sabrina-carpenter-interview-2023

Grammy History: https://www.grammy.com/artists/sabrina-carpenter/57838

Grammy.com, "Jack Antonoff's 'Grand Desire': Why Working With Taylor Swift, Sabrina Carpenter & Bleachers Is His Dream Creative Playground," September 2024: https://www.grammy.com/news/jack-antonoff-interview-working-with-taylor-swift-sabrina-carpenter-bleachers

HollyWire, "Sabrina Carpenter Gushes Over Rowan Blanchard + Talks Summer De-Tour + Secrets," June 2017: https://www.youtube.com/watch?v=BqCtKYEtnlc

Hot Ones, "Sabrina Carpenter Talks Nonsense While Eating Spicy Wings," July 2024: https://www.youtube.com/watch?v=msnI0D1SDSg

iHeartRadio, "Sabrina Carpenter—The New Album (Q&A on the Honda Stage at the iHeartRadio Theater)," September 2016: https://www.youtube.com/watch?v=n5CkYKTSRmI

IMDb: https://www.imdb.com/name/nm4248775/

Instagram: https://www.instagram.com/sabrinacarpenter/

Interview, "Sabrina Carpenter and Maya Hawke on Rethinking the Pop Star Playbook," February 2024: https://www.interviewmagazine.com/music/sabrina-carpenter-and-maya-hawke-on-rethinking-the-pop-star-playbook

Marie Claire, "Sabrina Carpenter Is Ready for Act II," June 2019: https://www.marieclaire.com/celebrity/a28184345/sabrina-carpenter-interview-2019/

"MileyWorld's 'Be a Star' Contest Round 5—Sabrina," October 2009: https://www.youtube.com/watch?v=YxlL5AAzsSk

NPR Music, "Sabrina Carpenter: Tiny Desk Concert," December 2024: https://www.youtube.com/watch?v=BEoGvTlJMyY

Nylon, "Roll Call: Meet 25 Gen Z'ers Changing The World," May 2018: https://www.nylon.com/life/roll-call-gen-z-list-nylon-may-2018-cover

Nylon, "Sabrina Carpenter Explains Why She's Not 'A Delicate Flower,'" May 2019: https://www.nylon.com/sabrina-carpenter-tribeca-interview

On Air with Ryan Seacrest, "Sabrina Carpenter Talks Opening For Ariana Grande in Brazil," July 2017: https://www.youtube.com/watch?v=j4wDA7m55Xs

Open House Party, "Sabrina Carpenter on Working With My Best Friends," February 2023: https://www.youtube.com/watch?v=TkbEFlEqcuM

People, "Sabrina Carpenter Reveals How Helping Out with the Ryan Seacrest Foundation Inspired Her," September 2016: https://web.archive.org/web/20160912133813/http://www.people.com/article/sabrina-carpenter-ryan-seacrest-foundation-inspired

People, "All About Sabrina Carpenter's Siblings, Cayla, Shannon and Sarah," February 2024: https://people.com/all-about-sabrina-carpenter-siblings-8598810

People, "All About Sabrina Carpenter's Parents, Elizabeth and David Carpenter," February 2024: https://people.com/all-about-sabrina-carpenter-parents-elizabeth-and-david-carpenter-8584964

People, "Why Sabrina Carpenter's Longtime Vocal Coach Wasn't Shocked by Her Turn to Sexier Lyrics (Exclusive)," December 2024: https://people.com/sabrina-carpenter-vocal-coach-eric-vetro-interview-exclusive-8766416

Radio Disney, "Sabrina Carpenter At Home," October 2016: https://www.youtube.com/watch?v=pPuSyjPeGA8&t=86s

Radio Disney, "Best of Sabrina Carpenter at Radio Disney," March 2019: https://www.youtube.com/watch?v=KMUsErRVYyU&t=424s

Recording Industry Association of America Achievements: https://www.riaa.com/gold-platinum/?tab_active=default-award&se=sabrina+carpenter#search_section

Rolling Stone, "Sabrina Carpenter 'Dealt with Perceptions.' Now She's Making Her Story Crystal Clear," July 2022: https://www.rollingstone.com/music/music-news/sabrina-carpenter-emails-i-cant-send-interview-1381304/

Rolling Stone, "Sabrina Carpenter Gave Us the Song of the Summer. She's Got a Plan for All Seasons," June 2024: https://www.rollingstone.com/music/music-features/sabrina-carpenter-espresso-short-n-sweet-taylor-swift-1235036627/

Rolling Stone, "Critics Called Sabrina Carpenter's Show 'Explicit.' Her Choreographer Backs Every Move," December 2024: https://www.rollingstone.com/music/music-features/sabrina-carpenter-choreography-jasmine-badie-juno-pose-1235174107/

Scholastic Ink Splot, "Sabrina Carpenter singer/songwriter and co-star on *Girl Meets World*," October 2014: https://web.archive.org/web/20160317042415/http://blog.scholastic.com/ink_splot_26/sabrina-carpenter.html

Teen Vogue, "Sabrina Carpenter Creates the Playlist to Her Life," July 2018: https://www.youtube.com/watch?v=5NahQrslgQ4&t=87s

Teen Vogue, "Sabrina Carpenter Shares Her Firsts," July 2019: https://www.youtube.com/watch?app=desktop&v=LTcuQnCxl_k&t=0s

Teen Vogue, "Sabrina Carpenter on Her Career, from 'Girl Meets World' to 'Work It,'" August 2020: https://www.teenvogue.com/story/sabrina-carpenter-girl-meets-world-to-work-it

The Guardian, "'I'm a tyrant!' Pop superstar Sabrina Carpenter on freakish fame, fighting Disney and writing the song of the summer," August 2024: https://www.theguardian.com/music/article/2024/aug/23/im-a-tyrant-pop-superstar-sabrina-carpenter-on-freakish-fame-fighting-disney-and-writing-the-song-of-the-summer

The Hollywood Reporter, "Sabrina Carpenter 'Had Literally No Idea' Anyone Would Like 'Espresso' Before It Came Out," December 2024: https://www.hollywoodreporter.com/news/music-news/sabrina-carpenter-dunkin-collab-espresso-new-music-1236095371/

The Late Show with Stephen Colbert, "Sabrina Carpenter Fell In Love With Paul McCartney After Hearing 'Rocky Raccoon,'" December 2024: https://www.cbs.com/shows/video/UHWvq9w9FzVht3epzhs4kUgb2LCfMH30/

Time, "Sabrina Carpenter Has Waited Her Whole Life for This," October 2024: https://time.com/7027418/sabrina-carpenter-interview-time-100-next/

USA Today, "Sabrina Carpenter brings sweetness and light to her polished, playful concert," October 2024: https://www.usatoday.com/story/entertainment/music/2024/10/06/sabrina-carpenter-concert-review-short-n-sweet-tour/75533197007/

Vanity Fair, "Sabrina Carpenter Creates Her Self Portrait," June 2024: https://www.youtube.com/watch?v=i6ALbJmMw_M

Variety, "Sabrina Carpenter on Taking Risks, 'Emails I Can't Send' Deluxe Edition, and Finally Performing 'Paris' in Paris," April 2023: https://variety.com/2023/music/news/sabrina-carpenter-emails-i-cant-send-fwd-1235574099/

Variety, "Sabrina Carpenter on Touring With Taylor Swift, 'Nonsense' Success and Scandalizing the Catholic Church: 'Jesus Was a Carpenter'," November 2023: https://variety.com/2023/music/news/sabrina-carpenter-touring-taylor-swift-nonsense-catholic-church-controversy-1235811476/

Variety, "Sabrina Carpenter Talks Getting Into the 'Mindset of a Slow Rise': 'I Am the Tortoise'," December 2023: https://variety.com/2023/music/news/sabrina-carpenter-hitmakers-speech-1235815391/

Variety, "Summer of Sabrina Carpenter: Hitting No. 1 on the Charts, Getting Advice From Best Friend Taylor Swift and What Barry Keoghan Really Thinks About Her Lyrics," August 2024: https://variety.com/2024/music/features/sabrina-carpenter-talks-top-charts-taylor-swift-barry-keoghan-1236096003/

Venice Music, "Sabrina Carpenter Marketing Case Study: Rebranding as a Superstar," (undated): https://www.venicemusic.co/blog/sabrina-carpenter-marketing-case-study-rebranding-as-a-superstar

Vogue, "Is Sabrina Carpenter the Next Selena Gomez?" November 2016: https://www.vogue.com/article/sabrina-carpenter-evolution-tour-coach-awards-celebrity-tour-style

Vogue, "Sabrina Carpenter on the Radical Honesty of Her New Album, *Emails I Can't Send*," August 2022: https://www.vogue.com/article/sabrina-carpenter-emails-i-cant-send-interview

Vogue, "'It Was Magic': Sabrina Carpenter Talks Kicking Off Taylor Swift's Eras Tour," August 2023: https://www.vogue.com/slideshow/sabrina-carpenter-taylor-swift-eras-tour-fashion

Vogue, "You're Welcome! An Exclusive Look Inside Sabrina Carpenter's 'Please Please Please' Music Video," June 2024: https://www.vogue.com/article/an-exclusive-look-inside-sabrina-carpenters-please-please-please-music-video

Vogue, "The business of Sabrina Carpenter," August 2024: https://www.voguebusiness.com/story/fashion/the-business-of-sabrina-carpenter

Vulture, "Why You Can't Stop Saying 'That's That Me, Espresso'," May 2024: https://www.vulture.com/article/sabrina-carpenter-incorrect-lyrics-espresso.html

W, "Sabrina Carpenter Knows She Has You Hooked," September 2024: https://www.wmagazine.com/culture/sabrina-carpenter-cover-interview-2024

Whowhatwear.com, "Becoming a Pop Star Was Sabrina Carpenter's Destiny," January 2024: https://www.whowhatwear.com/sabrina-carpenter-interview

WIRED, "Sabrina Carpenter Answers the Web's Most Searched Questions," December 2021: https://www.youtube.com/watch?v=54b3tCV3LFk

YouTube, JJ Ryan, "Stars In Cars With Sabrina Carpenter," July 2018: https://www.youtube.com/watch?v=qizkaAwmuYY

YouTube, Sabrina Carpenter Official Page, "Sabrina Chats 'Eyes Wide Open'," April 2015: https://www.youtube.com/watch?v=o95di894U3o

Zach Sang Show, "Sabrina Carpenter Talks Almost Love, Singular & Marshmello," June 2018: https://www.youtube.com/watch?v=c2FrKSKqM4Q&t=469s

SOURCES

Photo Credits

Page 2: © Jeff Kravitz/Getty images

Page 4: © Jamie McCarthy/Getty images

Page 6: © Maya Dehlin Spach/Getty images

Page 10: © PA Images/Alamy Stock Photo

Page 13: © Emma McIntyre/Getty images

Page 16-17: © Frazer Harrison/Getty images

Page 18: © Jeff Kravitz/Getty images

Page 24: © Mike Coppola/Getty images

Page 32: © Araya Doheny/Getty images

Page 37: © John Sciulli/Getty images

Page 39: © CBS Photo Archive/Getty images

Page 43: © Tony Rivetti/Getty images

Page 47: © Bruce Glikas/Getty images

Page 48: © Image Group LA/Getty images

Page 51: © Vincent Sandoval/Getty images

Page 52: © Jeff Kravitz/Getty images

Page 66: © Taylor Hill/Getty images

Page 70: © Edward Berthelot/Getty images

Page 73: © Dave Benett/VF24/Getty images

Page 77: © CBS Photo Archive/Getty images

Page 78: © Alexander Tamargo/Getty images

Page 85: © Noam Galai/Getty images

Page 88: © Corey Nickols/Getty images

Page 90: © Graham Denholm/TAS24/Getty images

Page 95: © The Photo Access/Alamy Stock Photo

Page 99: © Paula Lobo/Getty images

Page 100: © Gilbert Flores/Getty images

Page 104: © Emma McIntyre/Getty images

Page 110: © Vivien Killilea/Getty images

Page 113: © Mark Von Holden/Getty images

Page 121: © Kevin Mazur/Getty images

Page 122: © John Shearer/Getty images

Page 125: © Rebecca Sapp/Getty images

Page 126: © Kevin Mazur/Getty images

Page 131: © Emma McIntyre/Getty images

Page 138: © Kevin Mazur/Getty images

Page 144: © Taylor Hill/Getty images

Page 149: © Christopher Polk/Getty images

Page 153: © UPI/Alamy Stock Photo

Page 154: © Taylor Hill/Getty images

Page 157: © Astrida Valigorsky/Getty images

Page 162: © Samir Hussein/Getty images

Page 165: © Kevork Djansezian/Getty images

Page 166: © Jamie McCarthy/Getty images

Page 173: © ZUMA Press, Inc/Alamy Stock Photo

Page 176: © Gareth Cattermole/Getty images

Page 181: © Taylor Hill/Getty images

Page 182: © Samir Hussein/Getty images

Page 185: © Paula Lobo/Getty images

Page 186: © Richard Shotwell/Invision/AP

Page 191: © Evan Agostini/Invision/AP

Page 192: © Kevin Mazur/Getty images

PHOTO CREDITS

Acknowledgments

We may have never survived the tumultuous 2024 without something as mindless and fun as "Espresso." Much in the same way that a coffee break can provide a moment to relax and take a pause from life's stressors, so did Sabrina's uber-hit and mega album. As a fellow Taurus, I know all about the mindset of hard work that Sabrina has put into her career and can only commend her for sticking through it all to become an "overnight success ten years in the making." To my fellow music critics and journalists who finally gave the pop star her due, culture has you to thank too, and it all but proves why this job is so valuable.

About the Author

Selena Fragassi is a fifteen-year music journalist who is currently a featured contributor for the *Chicago Sun-Times* as well as *SPIN* and *Loudwire*. Her bylines have also appeared in *The A.V. Club*, *Paste*, *Nylon*, *PopMatters*, *Blurt*, *Under the Radar*, and *Chicago Magazine*, where she was previously on staff as Pop/Rock Critic. Artists she's interviewed include Rise Against, Gene Simmons, Jennifer Hudson, Andra Day, Chrissie Hynde, Demi Lovato, Debbie Harry, Slash, Deftones, Evanescence, Alice Cooper, Jack White, The Black Keys, Charlie Puth, Bon Jovi, and Bonnie Raitt, among many others. Selena's work has been anthologized in *That Devil Music: Best Music Writing* and she has appeared on televised panels regarding music matters for WTTW's *Chicago Tonight* program. She is the author of the books *New Kids on the Block 40th Anniversary Celebration*, *NSYNC 30th Anniversary Celebration*, *Greta*, and *Alanis Morrisette JLP 30th Anniversary* with more to come. Selena is also a voting member of The Recording Academy.

© 2025 by Quarto Publishing Group USA Inc.

First published in 2025 by Epic Ink, an imprint of The Quarto Group,
142 West 36th Street, 4th Floor, New York, NY 10018, USA
(212) 779-4972 www.Quarto.com

EEA Representation, WTS Tax d.o.o.,
Žanova ulica 3, 4000 Kranj, Slovenia.
www.wts-tax.si

All rights reserved. No part of this book may be reproduced in any form without written permission of the copyright owners. All images included in this book are original works created by the artist credited on the copyright page, not generated by artificial intelligence, and have been reproduced with the knowledge and prior consent of the artist. The producer, publisher, and printer accept no responsibility for any infringement of copyright or otherwise arising from the contents of this publication. Every effort has been made to ensure that credits accurately comply with the information supplied. We apologize for any inaccuracies that may have occurred and will address inaccurate or missing information in a subsequent reprinting of the book.

Epic Ink titles are also available at discount for retail, wholesale, promotional, and bulk purchase. For details, contact the Special Sales Manager by email at specialsales@quarto.com or by mail at The Quarto Group, Attn: Special Sales Manager, 100 Cummings Center Suite 265D, Beverly, MA 01915 USA.

10 9 8 7 6 5 4 3 2 1

ISBN: 978-0-7603-9929-3

Digital edition published in 2025
eISBN: 978-0-7603-9930-9

Library of Congress Control Number: 2025933858

Group Publisher: Rage Kindelsperger
Editorial Director: Erin Canning
Creative Director: Laura Drew
Managing Editor: Cara Donaldson
Editor: Katelynn Abraham
Art Director: Scott Richardson
Cover and Interior Design: Andy Warren Design

Printed in Huizhou, Guangdong, China TT072025

This book has not been prepared, approved, or licensed by the author, producer, or owner of any motion picture, television program, book, game, blog, or other work referred to herein. This is not an official or licensed publication. We recognize further that some words, models' names, and designations mentioned herein are the property of the trademark holder. We use them for identification purposes only.